Rory Hyde

Roy H

FOR DONNA! SEPT, 2012

Routledge
Taylor & Francis Group

NEW YORK AND LONDON

FUTURE PRACTICE

Conversations

from the Edge of Architecture

2012

FOREWORD
Dan Hill

The disruptive power of an edge

This is not a book of predictions. As physicist Niels Bohr once said, 'prediction is very difficult, particularly about the future'. This certainly now applies to trades as much as technologies. Occupations were once so static that we took our surnames from them: Smith, Cooper, Taylor, Potter…

Not any more. Today's combination of economic permafrost and pervasive volatility, peppered with black swans, means that even informed projections are more problematic than ever.

Either way, people within a profession are often least well placed to see the disruptive challenge or the 'adjacent possibles', as Steven Johnson puts it. Don't ask an architect about the future of architecture. Most won't know. Just as few journalists, say, will know the future of journalism, or few retailers will be able to contemplate the future of retail.

From within, it is difficult to even perceive, and so question, the deeper values, motives, models or possibilities for the profession; hence, many professional bodies tend to be slowly fossilising within the compacting strata of their habits, discourse, and silent assumptions. Entire professions are now susceptible to creative disruption.

So this is not a book of predictions. But in lassoing together a set of interesting people and arranging them to define an edge of architectural practice, from both within and without the profession, Rory Hyde is describing a set of possible trajectories nonetheless.

Those selected from inside architecture are amongst those within the profession most likely to retain a critical distance, most likely to be capable of rewiring the guts of the practice from within, most likely to genuinely take forward the idea of spatial intelligence and practice, forging new relationships and positions.

Dan Hill

Those drawn in from the other side offer up the most interesting connectors or alternatives, originating outside of architecture and free of its baggage, yet drawing from its history and practices when it is productive to do so.

'The disruptive power of an edge must be reckoned with'.[1]

We still won't know the x, y, z coordinates of this edge, and it is constantly moving. Yet designers at least have an almost instinctive way of finding out what the edge might mean, and that is to prototype. This book offers a set of half-drawn blueprints, half-formed thoughts, tentative experiments, contingent structures, and false memories of alternative trajectories; in other words, perfect material to prototype the new edges of architecture with.

Yet Rory's introduction to this publication starts with the word 'crisis' rather than opportunity. We've been here before. That word is strongly reminiscent of the title of a 1974 publication by Malcolm MacEwan, *Crisis in Architecture*.[2]

MacEwan described a profession labouring under a 'world economic crisis' as well as contributing to an ecological imbalance in terms of resource inefficiency in construction, whilst implicitly supporting the craven exploitation of land value and communities. He suggested 'a return to first principles and the release of the latent skills and energies that are now being misused or frustrated'.

It could've been written yesterday.

The business model is still a mess. Most architects are poorly paid or work long hours to impossibly tight margins, and those practices with high-profile projects seem to exist purely through a form of voluntary slave labour from interns. US-based research recently found that architecture graduates had the highest rates of unemployment, of all graduates.[3] (Even when they do gain employment, many will never actually work within the field of architecture.)

There has been no meaningful advance on architects working as developer/builders; source of income is still largely a percentage of construction fees, neatly limiting solutions to buildings, which is very limited indeed. In the main, business development means waiting for clients to ask. The trade is trapped in the 'build and sell, hit and run' model of development and construction, according to Hans Vermeulen of DUS Architects, leading to architects inadvertently becoming '"experts" in typologies that we will never be asked to repeat', as Rem Koolhaas once eeyore'd.[4]

There has been no meaningful innovation around product or service models, or genuine advances in mainstream construction technologies. The idea of architectural intelligence embedded in organisations is more redolent of the 1950s than the present day.

The lack of progress is mystifying, particularly as, again, we've been here before. Two decades before MacEwan was writing, in smoggy 1950s London, you could find the London County Council architecture department (a training ground for the Smithsons and Archigram) developing the notion of active and embedded design intelligence at the heart of government. You'd also find the hybrid model of Span Developments, positioning design excellence at the heart of architect-led property development, and the multidisciplinary Design Research Unit, a practice that combined architecture, graphics, and industrial design to eventually become one of Europe's largest design offices, and with a hand in shaping the fabric of everyday British life, from pubs, town centres and railways to the Festival of Britain.

However, over half a century on, we are still debating whether the potency of traditional architecture's core proposition – spatial intelligence – is overplayed. As Wouter Vanstiphout discusses here, the deeper strategy for the *banlieues* of Paris, and indeed our approach to cities in general, is more likely to hold the seeds of their destruction than the particularities of the built fabric, even despite the apparent '100% correlation' between Corbusian-inspired blocks and riots. That deeper strategy is not something architects currently get to engage with, or are particularly equipped to engage with. They are mainly perceived as working to create buildings and urban spaces, yet buildings are not why cities exist; they are simply a side-effect of cities.

Genuinely addressing urban strategy only partly involves spatial intelligence. Such strategies would benefit from a serious exploration of the craft of city-making, but there is no evidence to suggest that architects are necessarily well-placed to lead that work, at least currently. The interviews here suggest a new breed that have some productive sensibilities, but for most architects, a thorough recalibration of their craft would be required to warrant their involvement in more meaningful aspects of city-making, beyond building.

The desire, as Liam Young puts it here, for architects to 'set the agenda for builders and city makers (rather than) being beaten around by the planning legislation' is a laudable ambition, but must be earned. As the world became more complex, architecture's seat at the table was crowded out, as one voice among many.

But the conditions by which architecture has been marginalised – which have often been its own limited world-view and arrogance – must yet be understood and addressed. This does not let overly simplistic planners or consultants off the hook; both trades are yet to realise that city-making is more than working the numbers and is instead an evolving work of continual cultural invention. One profession's limitations are not an excuse for another's, however. Until the edges of architecture sketched out by this book, and in a few other places, are transformed into meaningful activities at the heart of the business, architecture will continue to get kicked, and rightly so.

Yet this book, and the emerging practices it describes, provide clues as to how to back out of the cul-de-sac that architecture has partly built, and most of them rely in some sense on an even deeper form of systemic integration and cross-fertilisation, supported by alternative business models.

'While continuity and visibility are crucial, strong edges are not necessarily impenetrable'.[1]

The interviews here do not suggest a return to 'first principles', in MacEwan's words. Going back to first principles would be, as Young points out here, 'a regression', and not a useful one. Instead, they are about figuring out 'next principles'. They may even suggest a set of principles for design practice wider than architecture. The joy in this book is in seeing the range of practices, approaches and services in play now, from inside and outside of these blurry, cross-hatched edges.

A practice like British firm BERG, essentially outside of architecture, and enjoying free reign in terms of business models and design practices, actually has much in common with the Design Research Unit. Similarly the ability to shape public opinion through crisp and engaging communication, as opposed to further withdrawing into the obfuscatory fug of 'archibabble', is shared by the likes of BERG, muf, DUS Architects, and many others here. As Conrad Hamann's reflection on the work of Robin Boyd makes clear, and particularly in Boyd's collaboration with *The Age* newspaper in creating the Small Homes Service, this too is a faint but consistent line drawn from the 1950s.

Most importantly perhaps, we are beginning to understand that there are certain characteristics required for this new work, one that often concerns spatial qualities but only as part of a wider brief, with different drivers other than

Dan Hill

the building.

Here, this role is often dubbed the 'professional generalist', a leader-type that must have the ability to talk convincingly with the wide range of people involved in a job – whether city, building, platform, product, service, business model – and then perform creative expertise in synthesis: projecting, not simply analysing; 'synthesysts' not analysts. They need to be able to design and deliver projects, and so work in multidisciplinary craft-oriented teams and contexts, as well as with users, but they must also zoom out of that production to survey the strategic scenario from 30,000 feet. They are constantly oscillating between the matter and the meta.

Some architects will be particularly good at this, given the necessity for orchestration, scale, strategy, context, abstraction, communication, decision-making and detail. Jeanne Gang is a great example here.

But this idea of the professional generalist is not exclusive to architecture. It's readily familiar to other design practices with a strategic bent and a multidisciplinary context, which are equally, if not more, complex: some architecture certainly, but also some urban and landscape design, some industrial design, some interaction design and service design, and so on. They also work in collaboration with other disciplines and approaches, such as those that have a deep understanding of people and their networks, such as psychologists, artists, economists, and sociologists, as well as whatever craft disciplines are relevant to the goal.

So while there is nothing particularly distinct and defining about architecture here, this is still a book about edges, and about an edge of architecture specifically. Yet the nature of edges means that it will also describe some 'not-architecture'.

With that in mind we should be aware of how both sides of that edge are articulated and personified. From just inside the edge marked architecture, we will find Steve Ashton, Robin Boyd, Mel Dodd, DUS Architects, Jeanne Gang, Indy Johar and Liam Young. Waving from the other side are Camila Bustamante, Natalie Jeremijenko, Bruce Mau, Matt Webb, and Marcus Westbury. A few stand on the edge itself, and could go either way: AMO, Bryan Boyer, Todd Reisz, Wouter Vanstiphout and *Volume*. It's a nicely balanced set, clustered around the edge whilst collectively pulling it further away from 'firmitas, utilitas, venustas', or the 'masterly, correct, and magnificent play of masses brought together in light'.

In describing the roles contained within this set, we discover a different view of this edge. Despite their playful nature, Rory's suggested 'shorthand' titles are both evocative and meaningful: yet they describe the edges of a practice that is design-wide, not just limited to architecture: 'Community Enabler', 'Contractual Innovator', 'Educator of Excess', 'Double Agent', 'Strategic Designer' …

Perhaps inadvertently, for instance, they're reminiscent of Norman Potter's descriptions of the functional roles designers play – 'culture generator', 'impresario', 'culture diffuser', 'assistant' and 'parasite' – in his seminal *What is a Designer*.[5]

It could be that there is a new kind of generalised design practice delineated by this edge, stretching across disciplines and contexts. Perhaps these 'vertical' distinctions between design disciplines derived from craft practices will become less important. Instead, design stratifies along a different axis – in effect horizontally – with a consistent kind of practice performed by strategic generalists and synthesists, engaged in cultural invention, higher-order question definition, multidisciplinary orchestration, disruptive change agency, and so on.

So the 'edge of *architecture*' outlined here might be common to other contexts. While that makes the subtitle of this book a touch misleading, this is certainly a good thing.

Architecture can still share the lead, though. When Bruce Mau describes the practice as largely predicated on 'synthesis informed by democratic civic values', he is also right to suggest that there may be 'nothing more important right now'. But it's the higher-order functions of synthesis, strategy and value creation that may be important, rather than the traditional craft of architecture as traditionally understood.

'Edges may also ... have directional qualities'.[1]

This is why it is relevant to look at the possibilities either side of this edge of architecture, encompassing, for example, non-architect Natalie Jeremijenko's alternative approaches of 'participatory research, participatory construction and open source' activism as well as the work of architect Bryan Boyer, who now sees the culture of public decision-making and the social contract as the design challenge. Boyer moves from inside to out, whereas Jeremijenko moves outside, in.

These wonderful ambitions clearly create a tension at the heart of our new idea of architecture. If an architect, trained in the craft skills of building and spatial intelligence, turns instead to re-shaping the social contract then which aspects of their practice were useful? If a non-architect can end up radically and systematically shaping places and spaces, what aspect of their development is most useful? And are great buildings and spaces a necessary enabler of new approaches, or simply a by-product of far greater strategies, systems and local cultures?

The tension is not resolved by this book. Architecture's core aim may still be the application of spatial intelligence, but if that outcome is not seen as valuable by the wider culture, then it doesn't solve two problems, one small, one big.

The first problem is architecture's marginalisation. This is not necessarily important in itself. Or at least, if the debates as to its value cannot be meaningfully resolved, it will only be of importance to architects.

But the second problem concerns how to access and deploy the considerable potential of architecture to solve genuinely meaningful and significant problems beyond the building. This one is important.

But it would be unfair to expect this book to neatly resolve these tensions, if not a little pointless too. These tensions generate the necessary friction required to generate debate, traction, and movement. What we need right now are a series of ambitious sketches indicating the edges of architectural practice, reinforced by case studies and role models amongst those who sit either side of those edges.

And that is what this book is for.

The nice thing about edges is that they lead to further edges. As you push through one edge, a shift in perspective reveals a further boundary on the horizon. The edges of architecture described in this book will have further edges on the other side; the pioneers talking here will have little sense of exactly what lies beyond the edge of architecture, as currently understood, but it is this curious and engaging mix of people both within and without the boundaries of the current profession that are best-placed to lead us there.

'Edges are often paths as well'.[1]

INTRODUCTION

Crisis!

The world today is defined by a constant state of crisis. From environmental degradation, ageing populations, financial instability, natural disasters, housing shortages, global migration, xenophobia, and a growing wealth disparity, to name just a few; our societies are increasingly challenged by systemic issues on an unprecedented scale. All of these crises have spatial consequences that architects are well prepared to confront, and yet instead of diving in, we seem to be having our own crisis: a crisis of relevance.

We complain of marginalisation from the process of real decision-making; of being treated like cake decorators only interested in styling; of being undervalued financially; of being over regulated; of being too exposed to the instability of the market, and more.

This foot-stamping isn't unwarranted. Only fifty years ago we were at the centre of the action. Massive reconstruction project? We had the answers. Population explosion? We had it covered. Environmental catastrophe? Solutions for that too. The post-war period in the Western world saw architects leading the way, enacting their theories for a better society on an unprecedented scale, shaping the world for the better.

Rory Hyde

Or so we thought.

Our visions for a clean, bright and optimistic future turned out to be anything but. Despite our best intentions, the very urban plans we laid out and buildings we erected in the name of progress, proved to be our downfall. The socially motivated urban developments of the post-war period came to represent poverty, social conflict, crime and depravity; leading many of them to be demol-

Demolition of the Pruitt-Igoe housing estate in St. Louis Missouri in 1972, only 17 years after its construction.

ished just to try and repair the damage they supposedly caused.

This crisis of architecture's responsibility for society sowed the seeds for our marginalised position of today. Could we ever be trusted to enact change on such a grand scale again? The 1980s and 1990s saw architects sheepishly retreat to the self-imposed exile of the drawing board, creating ever more abstract and autonomous visions, but not for society, for each other. This period also saw the rise of private development and the decline of public works departments, leading architects to follow the money into the commercial sector. Architecture became a key tool in real-estate speculation; a business product with an expectation to generate a return on investment, an obligation which inevitably led to the further erosion of architects' civic responsibilities.

Calls for a new kind of designer stretch back to the middle of the 20th century, most famously with Buckminster Fuller's 1963 description of a 'synthesis of artist, inventor, mechanic, objective economist and evolutionary strategist'.[6] A role that Bruce Mau has more recently embraced, acknowledging that the complexity of today's problems would necessitate that these roles be taken up by the 'collective intelligence of a team'.[7] MoMA curator of design Paola Antonelli calls for designers to adopt the role of 'society's new pragmatic intellectuals ... changing from form giver[s] to fundamental interpreter[s] of an extraordinarily dynamic reality'.[8] Critic and environmentalist John Thackara similarly calls for designers to 'evolve from being the individual authors of objects or buildings, to being the facilitators of change among large groups of people'.[9]

But with all of this demand for change, where are the results? Science fiction author William Gibson's dictum 'The future is already here – it's just not very evenly distributed' holds true in this case. While the mainstream may be slow to adapt, there are designers around the world eagerly carving out opportunities for new kinds of engagement, new kinds of collaboration, new kinds of practice and new kinds of design outcomes; overturning the inherited assumptions of the design professions.

This book compiles seventeen conversations with practitioners from the worlds of architecture, policy, activism, design, education, research, history, community engagement and more, each representing points on the ever-shifting edge of architecture, and offering potential futures for practice in the 21st century.

In focusing on non-traditional models of practice, by no means does this book set out to diminish the knowledge and expertise required to design and deliver a physical building. Architects today face an increasingly complex and contradictory array of expectations: every building must be green, cheap, marketable, conforming to regulations, on time, on budget, make money, and more often than not, be iconic. It is a culture that creates architecture, not just individuals, and we live in a culture that's increasingly motivated by investment, promoted by public relations, and regulated by the threat of litigation. In the face of these forces, every building of even modest scale or ambition is remarkable.

But what these conditions highlight is a fundamental shifting of the playing field. In order to navigate this new terrain productively we need fundamentally new models of practice. And the best place to start is to look at those operating on the edges of architecture today.

In Newcastle, Australia, a city hollowed out by a declining industrial sector and competition from big box stores on the periphery, the Renew project led by Marcus Westbury has kickstarted a revival by negotiating for vacant commercial spaces to be occupied by artists and creative businesses. Where millions spent on physical reconstruction had made little impact, this inexpensive strategy centred on people has led to a radical transformation.

In New York City, artist/scientist/environmentalist Natalie Jeremijenko has appropriated the role of health professional to offer prescriptions not for pharmaceuticals, but for public interventions. Jeremijenko's Environmental

Rory Hyde

Health Clinic reframes health as dependent upon external conditions, such as air quality, water quality, and exposure to animals, as opposed to our internal biology. By improving the ecosystems we live in, we have the potential to improve not only our own health, but to produce collective benefits, improving the health of an entire neighbourhood or even a city.

In London, architect and educator Liam Young runs the Unknown Fields Division, a unit of the Architectural Association which takes students to far-flung corners of the earth in an investigation of our relationship to landscape, technology and the future. By exploring beyond the traditional terrain of architectural production, Young and his students return with unique perspectives on our relationship with the planet and the environment, producing independent thinkers ready to face the challenges of the 21st century.

In Melbourne, architects Ashton Raggatt McDougall (ARM), known for their radical and experimental design, also conduct experiments at the drier end of architectural production: contracts. By drafting agreements which share the risk between the client, architect, and general contractor, the process of construction is

Introduction

transformed from being combative to cooperative, allowing ARM to deliver their risky projects
on time and on budget.

In Lima, graphic design student Camila
Bustamante, disillusioned with her hometown's
corruption and reluctance to invest meaningfully
in public infrastructure, launched a campaign to
raise public awareness. Focusing on Lima's metro
line, intended to be rolled out across the city
in the 1980s but which still today only consists of
four stops, Bustamante created signs for the
unbuilt stations with the year they would be completed at the current rate of progress. This simple
graphic intervention has returned the metro
to the public consciousness and contributed to
reviving the political impetus to proceed with
construction.

What unites each of these examples, and the
others explored in this book, is a questioning of
the traditional tools used to shape the city. Like a
hammer which can only see nails, architects
had become blind to other means of enacting
urban change; where, as Cedric Price points out,
'the best solution to an architectural problem
may not necessarily be a building'. The examples
drawn together in this book illustrate architects
operating beyond their capacity as building

23   Rory Hyde

design professionals, as 'custodians of the built environment'. Their concerns are broadly understood to be for the quality of the city as a whole, rather than the acquisition of new projects to fuel an office or leave an authored mark, forging a new era of civic responsibility and ethical entrepreneurialism.

The diverse geography of architectural and spatial practice today, with the architectural office as shrinking polar ice cap. 'The Architect's New Atlas' by Martti Kalliala and Hans Park.

BLUE OCEAN STRATEGIES

THE NEW ARCHITECTURAL PRACTICE

COMMUNICATIONS

Cinema

- Location Scout
- 3D Artist

Motion
Graphics
Designer

Gaming

- Game
  Designer
- Technologist

Wizard

- Editor
- Journalist

Book
Reviews

Media

- TV Host

Digital Set
Designer

Set Designer

Produce

Celebrity
Philanthropist

Art Director

Critic

Publisher

Design & Build

Re-configured
Architect

Cultural
Generalist

Think
Tank

Green
Activist

Master
Builder

Office
Partner

THE ARCHITECTURAL
OFFICE

Office
Architect

The Solo
Genius

GOVERNMENT

- MP
- Urban Warfare
  Officer
- Development
  Director

System Designer

President

Mayor

Policy Analyst

Spatial Advisor

Social Space
Expert

Project
Manager

Activist

Slum Upgrade
Specialist

Urban Youth
Specialist

CIVIL
SOCIETY

Urban post-conflict
coordinator

Public
Intellectual

Space Colony
Designer

ROGUE ISLANDS

Luxury

Energy
Conservation
Expert

Lighting
Designer

Real Estate
Developer

Construction
Management

BUILDING INDUSTRY

Seismic Designer

Mold Maker

Sustainability
Consultant

Acoustic
Designer

Environmental
Behavior Expert

Project
Manager

Plaza/Region
Brand Manager

Planner

Sustainability
Expert

URBANISM

Transport
Expert

Researcher

Teacher

Academia

Site Planner

Urban
Historian

EDUCATION

Museums

Professor

Researcher

Curator

Infrastructure
Planner

Urban
Designer

GIS Specialist

Exhibition
Designer

CAD Developer

CAD Planner

Director

Visual
Interaction
Designer

Usability
Expert

3D Visualizer

Urban Energy
Specialist

Virtual
Environments

TECHNOLOGY

BIM Expert

User Interface
Designer

3D Software
Developer

Crisis
Management

Evacuation
Planner

Disaster Mitigation
Coordinator

Reconstruction
Coordinator

Golf Course
Designer

Hospitality
Concept Designer

SPATIAL COMMODITIES

Real Estate
Broker

THE
MASSIVE
CHANGER

Bruce Mau

'Change'. On its own, it's a pretty powerful word. It implies progress, upheaval, transformation, ambition; and in the hands of Barack Obama, became nothing short of a rallying cry for an entire nation. Now add the word 'massive' in front of it, and these factors are magnified, likely to encompass the entire world and all the people in it. Indeed, Massive Change, Bruce Mau's ongoing project – encompassing exhibitions, radio, web, books and now a 'network' – is not short on ambition.

The germ of Massive Change is cited as a quote from historian Arnold Toynbee: 'The twentieth century will be chiefly remembered by future generations not as an era of political conflict or technical invention, but as an age in which human society dared to think of the welfare of the whole human race as a practical objective'. For Mau, the primary way to achieve this practical objective is through *design*. And we as designers, with our expertise in creative synthesis, have the responsibility to apply this expertise in shaping the world for the better.

So how are we faring? Well, according to Mau, architects in particular have dropped the ball. In an op-ed for *Architect* magazine, Mau chastises the profession for complaining of 'powerlessness, economic hardship, marginalisation and irrelevance', when there are real problems out there to be solved.[10] While Mau is chiefly known as a graphic designer, as a collaborator with architects including Frank Gehry, and having designed OMA/Rem Koolhaas' seminal monograph *SMLXL*, he holds a unique and authoritative perspective on what architects do.

Despite his criticisms, Mau remains 'famously optimistic' about the future. His book *Massive Change* covers advances in fields as diverse as transport, astronomy, economics, materials, energy, information, and yes, even architecture, which all offer cause for hope.[11] Some even offer hope for profit. Unlike many of the socially-motivated designers out there, Mau isn't shy when it comes to discussing money. He makes no illusions about what a potentially lucrative field 'redesigning the world' could be. Which has the dual benefits of presumably attracting people to the cause, and also shrugging off the self-righteousness that pervades much of the rhetoric of sustainability. Instead, challenges are reframed as opportunities: 'bad is good, terrible is awesome, that's the kind of people we are'.

With Mau's latest project, the Massive Change Network, his aim has shifted to spreading the message, to change the position and perception of design in the world, and to convince designers, policy-makers, business-leaders and citizens to embrace this manifesto and carry it into their field of work, and then of course, change the world. Seems like a fairly practical objective.

Conducted 14th December 2011 over Skype between Amsterdam and Chicago.

Rory Hyde: To start off, I wanted to ask you about this piece you wrote for *Architect* magazine, 'You Can Do Better',[10] where you launch a scathing attack on architects and their constant complaints. I just thought 'Wow', this is an important perspective. And of course it attracted plenty of negative comments – it clearly touched a nerve – which proved your point in a way.

Bruce Mau: If you think about architecture as a methodology – independent of the outcome, as agnostic from its product – you would see that architecture has a deep culture of synthesis informed by civic values. Whenever I talk to architects or work with architects, all the best ones – the ones you get really excited by and respect – they're civic minded. They have a set of values and a responsibility to culture, to society and to ecology. They think civically. So if you imagine synthesis informed by democratic civic values, there is nothing more important right now. If you have that capacity, that's the most valuable capacity of this time in history.

Bruce Mau

But you spent so much time policing the fence that you forgot to open the door. You were so focused on not letting anyone in who didn't have the credentials that you forgot to let people out. And what has happened is that design has really come into its own as the bigger voice, and architecture has become kind of notched-down in its impact and importance because of this regulatory obsession. This obsession with the boundary has constrained the capacity of architecture right at the moment when it's so important to extend beyond the boundary.

Working with architects like Rem Koolhaas or Frank Gehry or Jeanne Gang, they synthesise hundreds of inputs into one coherent experience. That's what we need to do today, that's the challenge of our new era: to synthesise incredibly complex inputs and reconcile those inputs into one coherent way of proceeding. And that applies to organisations, governments, businesses, manufacturing problems, product problems, intellectual problems, learning problems; I mean, this kind of methodology is the methodology we need to develop.

RH: How do we then reconceive of what we do? Architects in particular seem to be tied up in a relationship to capital that is perhaps running against this civic agenda that you talk about. Is it as simple as redefining who we work for or the terrains we operate in?

BM: I think that is true. The real invention of Massive Change was to disconnect the methodology of design from the visual, to look at design as the capacity to produce a specific future. One of the great challenges I face in doing the work that I'm trying to do is that when I say the word 'design', people think of singular authorship and fancy expensive things. They think 'OK, this is somebody doing things that are going to be really expensive'.

RH: As opposed to the kind of intelligence you can bring.

BM: Right, because actually the best design becomes invisible. If you think about the experience you have on an airplane, the degree to which it is invisible is the highest order of the accomplishment, because you actually don't want to experience the tonnes of high explosives you are sitting on and flying through the air. You don't want to experience the jet engine or how brilliant the design is, you actually want an experience that is focused on you. So the highest order is this invisibility and ubiquity, and most people don't think that stuff is designed. But there is a very high level of design that allows us to have that interaction.

If we talk about design in terms of developing capacity to produce positive futures, that's a very different outcome than if we define it as producing buildings. On the one hand the culture of architecture has this commitment to collective civic values and the process of synthesis, but it's also still haunted by Ayn Rand. It's haunted by the idea of superman, and so many people fall prey to this idea even though they know the reality of their work is different. So if you go into Frank Gehry's studio, it's an extraordinary group of people that make Frank Gehry possible, and in the same way, he made them possible. So there's a reciprocal relationship. Now I am in no way denying the talent of Frank Gehry, he's unique historically, but actually it's a collective work in a collective context.

Overleaf: Mau's critical repositioning: 'From the world of design, to the design of the world'.

Bruce Mau

I don't know if you have seen this, but Frank is putting together a consortium of people looking at the future of architecture, which I think is on the one hand quite promising, but I suspect what they are doing is developing better infrastructure to do architecture as it is currently defined. They want to do fancy expensive things more efficiently, instead of thinking about it completely differently.

RH: Well, this raises an interesting point. Just to play devil's advocate, the kinds of projects you are talking about require designers to expand their agenda beyond just making things look pretty, but then this is also related to how we get paid a lot of the time. Should we feel guilty if we are *just* designers?

BM: I think we should actually. I mean, I think we should feel guilty in the same way that a philosopher would feel guilty if they were working without thinking. The way that we are defining design is as a thinking practice, it's a conscious practice, and we should feel guilty if we are unconscious of the impacts that we are having, as unfortunately we're living in a time when we don't have that luxury. For most of history that would be perfectly fine; if you were a designer two hundred years ago and you didn't really care about anything, go right ahead, it's not a problem. There's one billion people, it doesn't matter, you can savage the landscape and move on. But there's no landscape left so you can't do that today without being intentionally problematic.

I like to flip it around and ask 'We have the capacity to make things compelling; what should we use that for?' I think the only way out of the challenges we face is through design. We are adding one million people a week to the planet, and if the average child is seven and a half pounds, that's seven and a half million pounds of flesh every week.

RH: That's a staggering statistic. And they're all growing and eating!

BM: That's right. And I can't find volunteers to get that number down. And that's the real challenge of our time. It's not actually climate change, climate change is a result of this problem. Whether we caused climate change or not is irrelevant, the way we will solve the problem is to design new ways of living to accommodate our new scale. And we are a million miles away from that, and there is nothing but opportunity. There's huge money to be made in doing it; the people who solve these problems will create the wealth of the new era.

RH: It's probably useful to now discuss your efforts to tackle these challenges through the work you're doing with the Massive Change Network, and this transition you've made from a designer in a studio to more of a public figure spreading the word. In particular I'm interested in this word 'network' and what that means in terms of how your organisation is put together.

BM: I think you're onto the key idea, which is *network*. A little over a year ago I stopped working in the studio, I'd got to a certain point in my work where it wasn't satisfying for me for a lot of reasons, I'd done it for twenty five years and it just became time. And we saw this other opportunity around education and design that needed to be developed, and as we got into the research we discovered that less than one percent of the world's population has had access to education beyond high school. And just think of the revolution of possibility that we've produced with this tiny fraction. When I first read it I was just like 'That can't be true! Is it true?' [laughs] Most people think it's between twelve and twenty percent, and you realise wow, they're off by an order of magnitude.

RH: That's incredible, it reframes our position as a responsibility.

BM: Yes. We realised that we were facing the wrong direction, we were looking at the one percent and we needed to turn around and look at the ninety nine percent, to think about putting the tools in their hands and allowing them to produce their future. We know from networks and collaborations and from the distribution of power and capacity what we have already achieved with one percent, and if you double that you're still only at two percent. So we realise that our project is to design a network and design the tools to distribute this capacity. That's what we're really focused on now. It's very exciting and also a little overwhelming. It's only been a year, but already we're starting to get some traction.

RH: It sure is an ambitious undertaking, just the sheer numbers involved. One of the strategies you seem to be using to tackle this scale is education. Through setting up the Institute Without Boundaries, the Centre for Massive Change, and now the Network which is also focused on workshops and learning experiences, how are you rethinking education?

BM: When we did the Institute Without Boundaries, we had eight or ten students, and when I moved to Chicago I was thinking of doing something quite similar. We were talking to some of the universities – I'm on the faculty at Northwestern – to set up a bigger version of that. But I had a young guy working for me and he said 'You know, you're really old fashioned', and I said 'Not too many people tell me that, I'm kind of famous for not being old fashioned actually!' [laughs] But I asked him what he meant by that, and he said 'Well, you're doing it like Michelangelo did it, it's the model we've used for hundreds of years. You're talking to a very small number of people, but there's a hundred thousand kids in India who know your work, they love what you do, and they're never going to get to spend a year with you, and you're telling them they can't be part of the new world'. It kind of blew me away, I had to start over. It was an incredible blind spot, I didn't see it. Basically what he said was you should apply Massive Change to education; don't just do it in the way that it's always been done before.

So in education, your job is not to deliver the content, because you already have the content. Content is all available now. What you're really delivering is the experience of how to manipulate this content. We call it a 'lost in the woods' methodology, because when you're lost in the woods, everything in the environment is important; it is information that is live and is relevant and can help you get out. That's what a designer does. A designer starts lost in the woods and has a methodology or orientation to get to a destination. That's what an entrepreneur does.

So if you think about this as actually a methodology for entrepreneurial design learning, you are really developing a design methodology of leadership. Design is about imagining the future and systematically working to execute that future. Well, if you look up 'leadership' in the dictionary it's going to say something like that, that's what leadership is. So if you think about design as leadership methodology, it goes back to your earlier question, 'Should we feel

Bruce Mau

guilty if we are unconscious?' Yeah actually, because you have a leadership role and you have to accept the responsibility of leadership and exercise that responsibility in order to contribute the most. That's what we're working on.

RH: It also seems that in order to be leaders or entrepreneurs, we will increasingly need to be able to engage more and more disciplines and specialists. In your lecture in Brisbane[12] you said 'the real challenges we face will not be won by technology or art, mathematics or poetry, but by putting these things together again'. Will these new design leaders actually be generalists able to integrate various fields of expertise?

BM: Absolutely, there is an expertise to synthesis. And having the capacity to connect with people across disciplines is super critical right now, because as I said, we won't solve the problem just by developing the solution. I mean, we have many solutions to many of the challenges we face, but if they are not compelling and exciting, and if they don't touch you in some way emotionally, you will turn away. So one of the concepts we discuss in our workshops is to 'compete with beauty', and the idea is basically that the way we will win is to make smart things sexy. To make smart things more beautiful than the stupid old way that we used to do it.

I take them through a speed primer on ten key dimensions of formal design [laughs]; it's not going to make you a design master, but if you have those ten ideas you can work with a formal designer. If you are running an organisation, suddenly you have a language to think about design in your organisation. Contrast, shape, colour – these are all ideas that have relevance in an organisation, just as they do in a formal outcome.

RH: Just to wrap up perhaps, I have one question about your outlook for the future and in particular on the effect of the crisis on your agenda. On the one hand, it seems like issues such as sustainability are now off the political agenda as we focus on the economy and employment for instance; we seem to have put aside any other social responsibilities. But on the other hand, people also seem to be interested in exploring fundamental new ways of structuring the way we do things and the way we build our societies. Are you optimistic about where we are headed or do you feel like you are really fighting against it?

BM: No, I'm actually very optimistic. I make a distinction and a personal commitment to have fact-based optimism. Because I think that without fact-based optimism you simply wouldn't do anything, you would just give up. I once had a funny exchange with David Byrne from Talking Heads about this, because he accused me of being optimistic.

RH: The nerve! [laughs]

BM: And I said 'David, look at your own work; if you weren't optimistic you wouldn't do what you do. You wouldn't start a world music label, you wouldn't do Talking Heads, you wouldn't do movies, you wouldn't do art'. When you do things, even the person with the most negative articulation is optimistic that it will improve things, otherwise they would just kill themselves or forget about it. So starting with fact-based optimism is really critical; if we weren't optimistic we wouldn't solve problems, and we do need to solve them.

As I pointed out, we are bringing a million children into the world every week; in a decade that's twenty-two Australias under the age of ten. Imagine! So we have to solve those problems, and we can't solve them if we are not optimistic. I mean it's not like there aren't challenges and problems and crises and dilemmas, but history shows us that we have an absolutely extraordinary capacity to invent and to design new solutions. So I've become kind of famously optimistic [laughs], but I am optimistic because I think that in times of crisis, change becomes possible.

THE CIVIC ENTREPRE NEUR

Indy Johar

00:/

The interview hasn't even begun and I've already been challenged. As I'm explaining the concept of this book, Indy Johar interjects, 'Well, firstly I would disagree with your title; we're not at the edge, we're at the centre!' This would become a recurring theme throughout our conversation, as Johar describes 00:/ (pronounced 'zero zero'), the practice he co-founded, and how each of their projects manifests the thinking of the emerging world we live in. According to Johar, the most critical narrative today is the shift from the command-and-control approach of the industrial age to the distributed, shared, intelligent and networked ecosystems of the information age. This is definitely not a niche market – an 'edge' – but simply the way things will be organised in the very near future.

This 21st-century agenda plays out on all scales of 00:/, from the way the organisation is structured, the various disciplines they engage, and the projects they develop. Founded in 2005 in London by (reluctant) architects Johar and David Saxby, 00:/ is a co-operative practice that engages a diverse range of skill-sets – from economists and anthropologists to coders and architects – to create projects that pursue their agenda of economic, social and environmental sustainability.

One of their latest projects, under development in Marylebone, is the Scale-Free School, where the capital- and carbon-intensive construction of a new school is eschewed by instead building on *social* capital. By drawing upon existing facilities throughout the neighbourhood – such as sports fields, libraries, cinemas and cafés – the school house as a singular place is instead re-imagined as a distributed network of people and places, all linked together with the dynamic and location-aware capacities of smart phones.

What this and many other of 00:/'s projects express is their concept of the 'Civic Economy', described as 'comprising people, ventures and behaviours that fuse innovative ways of doing from the traditionally distant spheres of civil society, the market, and the state'.[13] Indeed, the words 'civic' and 'economy' don't often go together: one represents the generous space of the public, the other of the self-interested space of private enterprise. And this is perhaps the most radical contribution of 00:/: it is focused squarely on generating outcomes, and isn't bogged down in the party political rhetorics of left or right. Their recent publication *Compendium for the Civic Economy* even includes a preface by Conservative UK Prime Minister David Cameron, an unlikely alliance given the general criticism of Cameron's 'Big Society' for seeking to place the burden of public services onto the shoulders of communities. Johar explains Cameron's preface as being 'a significant and useful opportunity to legitimise the debate at that level'. Indeed, the projects included in the *Compendium* show alternate and constructive precedents for the Big Society in action.

When viewed as architects, 00:/ are way out on the edge, engaging disciplines and strategies that are foreign to 'traditional' practice. But with this ability to attract support from the highest levels of government, 00:/ place themselves firmly at the centre of an emergent reality, one that's just around the corner.

Conducted 29th November 2011 over Skype between Amsterdam and London.

Rory Hyde: I came across a video of a debate hosted by the Architecture Foundation[14] about the role of architecture in the crisis, where you said you 'would reluctantly call yourself an architect'. So with that in mind, what do you see is wrong with the title 'architect', if anything, and how might you define yourself otherwise?

Indy Johar

Indy Johar: I don't think the challenge is the term 'architect', I think it's the unfortunate professional and institutional infrastructure and the values associated with it. In fact, I think architecture is going to become more and more powerful as we move away from the idea of management and toward creating conditions for behavioural nudges, self-organisation, and a deep influence on systems; physical environments and the ambient structuring of spaces will play a powerful role in this. But I think the way we've trained architects and the institutional body around architecture is just *redundant*, and we need to dissociate the two.

The systemic problem is that the internal debate is focused on the image and semiotics of architecture – the image as a tool to raise capital financing for buildings – it was the 'iconic' nature which was seen as the key driver of architecture. On the other hand, we had the counter movement, the tectonic movement which fetishises the act of construction. Unfortunately, neither of those approaches are actually about the performative impact or the institutional behaviour of those environments.

There are very low levels of behavioural understanding in architecture. The models that architects produce are physical, spatial models; cardboard models of the frame. It's like Picasso turning around and saying 'Here's the frame of my painting, would you mind buying it?'

RH: What sort of tactics or approaches are you using in your practice to redress this balance, or to try and bring architecture back to a more human-centric approach? In particular you mention the importance

The Civic Entrepreneur

of working with various different disciplines beyond architecture.

> IJ: Somebody asked me just this morning whether I knew anyone in Vancouver doing 'architecture, design, placemaking and economics?' And I thought it was interesting that they were her four criteria; it was the fusion of those things which she thought we did. Our capabilities came out of being part of the policy think-tank world, as well as the design world, so there are fundamentally different disciplines at the heart of the team. We've got some fund managers sitting here, we've got urban geographers, we've got anthropologists, we've got coders, so actually the background of the team is very diverse. We do build things, we also do research – real research – and we also host forums, so you actually have to do all three. I think the richness of the team is one of the key aspects of that as well.

RH: I was speaking to the Helsinki Design Lab team at Sitra a few weeks ago, and they speak of how the policy is really important, the programming is really important, but it also needs to have a spatial aspect to be able to really communicate the idea. I'm interested in how you might approach doing a real building, or is that something you're less interested in these days?

> IJ: No no, we're doing lots of real buildings. I actually think that dichotomy of doing a real building or not is part of the problem. The challenge is not whether you do a real building or not, the challenge is whether you are making places better. The language default is a problem. I can spot an architect when he walks into The Hub because they say 'Oooh, nice space', and I think 'Yeah, you're missing the point'.

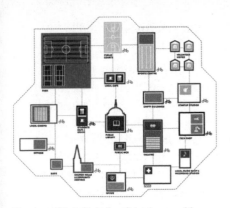

Diagram of 00:/'s Scale-Free School proposal for a campus distributed throughout existing buildings and services of a neighbourhood.

We are about to finish a £4.5 million building in Sheffield, we are doing a new super low-energy dorm for a girls school, we've just done several hyper low-carbon houses, we're developing the WikiHouse, we're doing a new decentralised school called the Scale-Free School in Marylebone which will be a mixture of institution and physical environment, we did The Hub, all the tables here are open-source tables done on CNC routing, based on a wiki platform.

RH: Sorry, I take it all back! So you really are tackling the full spectrum and delivery.

IJ: That's right. Sometimes I have to list all those projects just to remind people. I suppose the problem with the question of whether we do buildings or not is that it's the wrong way of framing the discourse. Yes, we do built environment – we think built environment is key – but that's not the focus of it. The focus is the outcome, and we happen to do built environment if that's what's required.

RH: One of the other themes in your work I'm really interested in is your approach to economy. I found a quote, where you say: 'It's time for architects to start reading the financial papers'.[15] You seem to take it much more seriously than many architects or other people in this space. Economics is a territory that's normally relegated to the developer or clients, we don't seem to worry about the money except how much the building costs. How do we reclaim this territory? Is it about getting involved with business models, business plans, thinking about how this thing might make money?

IJ: *It's all the same act.* The idea that we can disassociate one aspect from another aspect is an illusion. It's an illusion of a 17th-century Enlightenment model, where we figured out that we could deal with the world in vitro, you could take architecture and isolate it, you could take the business model and isolate it, you could isolate different components, and say 'Hey, if we isolate it, we can deal with it in effective ways'. That is an Enlightenment model of how you organise the world. Now, what is becoming apparent in the world we're living in, is that in vitro modelling of the world isn't able to cope with the complexity, i.e. the externalities all those models were generating. So carbon is just an externality of a model which doesn't take account of certain things. It's an in vitro business model. That's the more fundamental problem, that I think we've reached the end of this siloed idea of building stuff. That's the systemic issue.

We are talking about building ecosystems where there are no hard divisions between the built environment, the value model, between the impacts it has, between how it absorbs carbon, what materials it uses – it's about seeding an organism, and I don't think you can make such hard distinctions between things. I always use the term 'design venturing'; I think great entrepreneurs seem to be pretty good designers frankly, they tend to have a very good eye for those things, because they use the same skills. So I think it's about this method of how you build systems, the 'architecture of systems', as opposed to the 'architecture of brick buildings'. That shift is one of the big things we are seeing, because this in vitro modelling doesn't work.

RH: It's probably useful to talk about your *Compendium for the Civic Economy* now, as it seems to be the perfect manifesto of that idea of the spatial and economic ecosystem. What is the 'Civic Economy', and do architects have a role to play in it?

IJ: In a sort of high-level sense the Civic Economy is an idea about how technology and a deep democratisation of process is liberating a new way for people to organise themselves locally, and to actually create institutions and organisations which are fundamentally focused on a civic purpose. They can be for-profit, not-for-profit, it doesn't really matter. It's a new citizen method of organising micro acts which can create a virtuous social, environmental and economic cycle. So whether it's the sixty-eight FabLabs all around the world, The Hub, or Community Kitchens, all these projects in the book are about the synthesis of social capital and investment capital to create a performative impact.

Now, the role of architects is huge, but it's about place-making as opposed to the design of a physical product. Hosting and creating those flows and networks, seeding them, and allowing them to iterate, is what the 21st-century architect will be doing, which is hugely significant. This is acutely democratic in terms of influence and power – there is going to be no single leadership, but democratic leadership. So I think the role of the architect is hugely significant, I just think it's a new type of architect. And I think this is part of a longitudinal trend, this democratisation of

The Civic Entrepreneur

capital, democratisation of power, democratisation of leadership, and this post-management world is opening up all sorts of new challenges.

RH: This new '21st-century architect' you're describing also seems to directly plug into the crisis of the economy at this moment. Architects were the first ones to lose their jobs really – our work had become so dependent on capital, financing and banks that we've been forced to rethink how we operate. So, is this new architect as civic entrepreneur an... *opportunity*?

IJ: Yes and no. The reason why I dislike the word 'opportunity' is that it sounds like it's a new way to capitalise ourselves. I think the civic entrepreneur is the genuine space of interaction and creation of value. I think it's the genuine space of how we will almost certainly be operating and hosting those new value networks and allowing them to emerge. For example, there are some great guys out in Cardigan in Wales who are building a new jeans factory. Are they architects? Yeah, because they are building a whole new idea of a factory by deeply embedding it within an ecosystem, by using permaculture methods; it's going to require different innovation process, different design process, different synthesis process. So actually we are seeing new forms of this stuff starting to emerge.

I think what we are seeing is the reemergence of the thinker and maker being fused again, and I think it's this fusion where architecture is at. Some of these people may not call themselves architects, but they play that same role of fusing thinking and making, and creating a new capacity of doing. But to make this

Indy Johar

shift will require us to genuinely let go of the past and embrace a near future.

RH: One of the things I think is great about the book, is that it puts this word 'economy' right up there front and centre. A lot of the community development world seem to be very cautious of this word, it's somehow associated with something they are trying hard to counter. But then you present this fantastic project by the Fintry Development Trust,[16] where a community has pulled together to purchase a wind turbine as part of a larger array. For me that really feels like the future, it shows that a community can do more than just oppose something or make a shared garden, it can actually engage on the scale of infrastructure, economy, and real energy.

IJ: Exactly, and what it's starting to show is the creative capacity. If we talk about Hardt and Negri's concept of the multitude, this is showing the generative capacity of the multitude, and that's also what is starting to be unleashed. We're creating new methods of organising ourselves, of organising investment, talent, capabilities and possibilities with space, and being able to create genuinely low-cost and low-governance but high-value models of financing around that, and return on investment for communities. So, for me there is something quite potent starting to happen.

RH: One of the projects from the book you've been leading directly is The Hub. This seems to be a core ongoing project for the studio, and you're even sitting in the brand new one in Westminster right now, which is something. What is The Hub, and what kind of people are working there? There also seems to be a

The Civic Entrepreneur

unique funding model which is central to its operation.

IJ: In its simplest sense The Hub is a platform to encourage autonomy and new forms of business. It's a platform with four layers: a physical environment which is biased towards being pro-social, operating in a connective capacity; there is an investment platform, which is about investing in the start-ups and the ideas that are happening

The Hub Westminster, one of a number of shared workspaces established by 00:/ as 'platform[s] to encourage autonomy and new forms of business'.

in that environment; there is a learning environment, which is a night school that will be announced later this year; and then we have a journalist on the books, so there's a media platform. For me, in the high-level sense, it's about saying the modern corporate won't be about the singular aim being executed, but about how the corporate shifts platform behaviour, and supports many people's aims. And the purpose is that they have an aim but they also have an economy of scale and the infrastructure provided.

RH: Another project I'd like to discuss is WikiHouse, which has created quite a positive buzz. When you first announced it a couple of months ago and I checked out the website – I guess it must have been its first iteration – there was this very interesting but simple structure for making a little room out of CNC milled pieces of plywood, but checking back again today it really makes sense as a *platform*, as something which is about sharing and networking, and which has a global reach. Perhaps you could talk about the big idea behind WikiHouse, and in particular, what problem is it solving?

IJ: One of the things we realised was that we are seeing a longitudinal trend of production moving from factories all the way down, and what we are going to see is the nature of production moving down lower and lower, more local and local. The tables in The Hub were manufactured in the space, they were all CNC routed, we are open-sourcing all the designs, so we are creating an almost DIY open IKEA model. We did this first with tables, we tried it out, it's a very interesting aesthetic – almost Japanese joinery meets digital tech – and very interesting in what it does to the nature of making. We were exploring this, but as

soon as you move into a post-authorship model, which is not about owning a particular intellectual property or a particular domain, and you move into the notion that this generative model means that people can use some of the details and technology, you start to create something which is quite fast and collaborative.

Construction of WikiHouse prototype, an 'open-source construction set'.

Now, the WikiHouse is what I call a 'poem of the future'. One of the things our practice has really struggled with was finding an aesthetic or tectonic that reflects our way of thinking. It was probably the first time we came to a tectonic structure where effectively we were able to create a product, open-source it and simultaneously digitally print it, to create something where the manufacture and construction can pretty much be done by lay people. So it's a start at creating a hyper-democratised mode

The Civic Entrepreneur

of making by actually sharing that making with many, many people, to try and iterate that model and transform it. In a sense, it allows us to tap into a zeitgeist of doing.

Until now there has been an articulation between the professional designer-maker and the amateur, what this is trying to do is create that smooth curve between these two positions – between the long tail and the high tail. By blurring that boundary you can do things which historically have not been done before.

RH: It's really fascinating, I like this idea of blurring between the 'pro' and the 'am'. It feels like you are trying to do with space what HTML has done to web design. It let everyone and their cat be able to contribute to the web by designing a website. And what's interesting is that this doesn't actually dent the value of the professionals, but only expands the tail of access.

IJ: Exactly. I don't think WikiHouse will undermine architecture, I think it will genuinely create a new collaborative infrastructure for architects and designers to work together. Whether WikiHouse works as an idea doesn't really matter; we did it, we're doing it, and it's growing. I don't think we should be fixated around our solution or anyone else's solution, and we hope other people will take this on and make it better. These are little things which show what's possible, that these technologies are possible. Right now we're looking at whether we can make an entire building refurbishment using open-source plans, all the cutting patterns, everything. Can we do that? Let's see how far we can push the model.

THE WHOLE-EARTH ARCHITECT

Reinier de Graaf & Laura Baird

AMO

Finnish architect Eliel Saarinen (1873–1950) viewed the construction of space as a continuous series of nested scales of operation, famously stating 'always design a thing by considering it in its next larger context – a chair in a room, a room in a house, a house in an environment, an environment in a city plan'. It's an elegant statement, placing useful limits around the relevant spatial context to consider when designing. But what happens when the context becomes intangible? How does this statement hold up in today's globalised world, where issues of identity, politics, environmental and commercial contexts pervade every scale of operation? Can architecture liberate itself from the scale of the building in order to remain relevant within this larger context?

This liberation is most clearly asserted by AMO, the research studio and think-tank of Rem Koolhaas' Office for Metropolitan Architecture (OMA), which 'applies architectural thinking in its pure form to questions of organisation, identity, culture and program'.[17] The diversity of AMO's projects – spanning publications, corporate identity, nation branding, education, clothing, and self-initiated speculative research – would seem to be evidence of the independent

Reinier de Graaf & Laura Baird

viability of expanding the scope of architectural production into these new territories. This signals a potential future for design practice directed not only toward architectural production, but also toward architectural thinking applied in its broadest sense.

This model also offers a way around one of the most self-defeating constructs of the architectural profession: charging as a percentage of construction cost, an antiquated fee structure that does little to justify the thinking and intelligence embedded in the architectural process. The inability to distinguish conceptual value from production-focused value that this model implies, also means we are not natural candidates for projects that require the approach of an architect, but that may not result in a building, a territory which AMO more than anyone can lay claim to.

The following interview with director of AMO Reinier de Graaf and AMO team member Laura Baird explores a number of projects they and the office are currently engaged with. From the Cronocaos exhibit at the 2010 Venice Architecture Biennale, which examines architecture and its preservation; the Strelka Institute, a new post-graduate school in Moscow for which

AMO have designed the curriculum; to Roadmap 2050, a plan for the drastic reduction of carbon emissions across the entire continent of Europe.

The Roadmap 2050 project, more than any other, demonstrates another advantage of liberating architecture from the obligation to construct: it is no longer constrained by the scale of the building. Having made this jump, the whole world becomes available as a subject, with all its complex issues and intriguing terrains as potential zones of operation. Architecture is free to actively propose solutions to the challenges of today, to go where it is needed, instead of waiting to be invited to act.

Conducted 27th August 2010 at the 12th Biennale of Architecture in Venice.

Rory Hyde: OMA's presence at the Venice Biennale this year is fairly comprehensive; your office even issued their own mini guide to the Biennale for those of us purely dedicated to all things OMA.

> Reinier de Graaf: It's largely designed to compensate for a very long absence at Biennales. At one stage we tried to make a point by being absent, so then if you're present, you have to make a point of being present. There is always a form of exaggeration either way.

RH: We have the launch of Strelka, we have your presentation of Roadmap 2050, and we have the major exhibit Cronocaos. I guess pervading all of these projects – and something which pervades the office generally – would be the word 'research'. At once it seems so obvious that this would be what architecture is focused on but in the hands of OMA, simply endeavouring to *understand the world* seems like a radical proposition. How can this be possible in the context of architecture?

> RdG: The thing is, we are interested in anything that affects our profession in the end, because we are always interested in breaking architecture's hermetic mould, and in a way it's about knowing you will profess architecture differently once you are more aware of everything that surrounds it and affects it. And I think this was important in how we defined the research themes for Strelka, but really 'an attempt to understand the world' as a description feels far too generic and far too pretentious at the same time.'

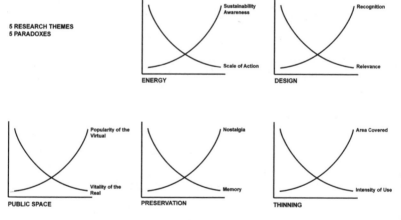

Concept diagram for curriculum of Strelka Institute for Media, Architecture and Design, Moscow.

The Whole-Earth Architect

RH: Well, to talk more about Strelka then, it's an incredible responsibility to design the curriculum for an architecture school; what kind of architects are you going to create in Russia?

RdG: I'm not sure you could say we're going to create architects... It's a school for Media, Architecture and Design – which together spells the acronym MAD – and it's post-graduate, so the architects we will turn out will have been architects even before they went in. We will turn out people with a certain amount of knowledge about particular subjects which are pressing. Also, because the school doesn't have an officially recognised degree, what we're trying to do is, in the span of a course, actually create a 'product'; a product which can be disseminated through the Strelka media network, which will then take the place of a degree. So you don't have a degree to show for your presence, but there is something you will have done on a certain product which you can show, which I think is increasingly important if you look at the way the job market in the architectural world works.

Laura Baird: And I think it also goes back to your question about the importance of research to our office; it's not a traditional architecture school in the sense that there is a design project and you present a building at the end of the semester. The product that we're looking to get is really research based, which may not necessarily have a physical presence or a proposed physical presence, it just has a conclusion.

RdG: Well, it's stronger than that, because while design is a theme, we don't teach design as a skill, we will deliberately teach design as a research subject. So we will analyse things through design, but we will also hopefully look at the world of design, how that

Reinier de Graaf & Laura Baird

world operates and do a kind of zoom out and there-fore maybe an X-ray of the state of the profession.

RH: This idea that what you might produce is not a building or that you may not teach design as a skill is also really clear in the preservation exhibit Crono-caos, where unlike many of the other pavilions there is no architecture on display; well there is, but it's not the main event.

RdG: But there are projects on display, because the thing about the preservation issue is that there are projects which go back in the history of our office – occasionally more than twenty years back – which are now in hindsight explained under the banner of preservation, even though we didn't consciously call it that at the time. Even in the type of commissions we get as an architectural firm, preservation as a theme has been relevant for quite some time. And there are quite a few projects, so in that sense it does deal with design and design solutions etc. But the kind of weird thing about preservation is that it also required look-ing at our own archive quite extensively. So we have the House in Bordeaux in there, which despite being a very recently produced building, is already a pro-tected monument; it has already been made subject to that regime. So in a way preservation is *chasing* design production and it's coming eerily close. The whole point of the exhibition is that preservation at some point becomes so close that it *overtakes* design, and then of course you have to decide in advance what you're going to keep and what you're not; the retrospective activity becomes a prospective activity.

RH: You've essentially observed this bizarre condition where we have this incredible appetite for preserva-tion in parallel with an appetite for destruction, and both of them seem to be guided by arbitrary forces which are having huge implications for the future of our cities, because, as I understand it, these decisions are very hard to roll back.

RdG: They are very hard to roll back and therefore their arbitrariness becomes all the more daunting. We did the Commonwealth Institute project in London which was actually a project about development: having to build a residential project – i.e. real estate to generate money – to have the money to actually pay for the preservation of an old 1960s building that couldn't pay for itself. And that in a way shows how development and preservation have to go extremely hand-in-hand, sometimes even on a shared site. In the course of that project we looked at London; the London of the 1960s and 1970s still invokes a major trauma. Some of the buildings from this period are listed, and some are demolished. So we studied which were kept and which were destroyed, and really with our best efforts we could not discover a pattern other than randomness, it just looked like 'OK, every third one has to go', and in that sense it is a very worrying thing because the more preservation is extended to the recent past, the less conceptual distance we have to make value judgements.

LB: The other nice thing about the preservation exhibit is that it doesn't just span the preservation of buildings. It's the preservation of space, it's the preservation of an urban condition… Rem wrote about Lagos and how to preserve this urban junk space.

RH: And furniture.

RdG: Yes, from the Haus der Kunst.

RH: I found this one of the most compelling and confronting contributions to the exhibit; to include the items of furniture that Hitler commissioned when he first came to power, which have since been recovered.

Preservation proposal for Libya, on a table commissioned by Adolf Hitler, collection of Munich's Haus der Kunst.

RdG: I have to say in all fairness the preservation exhibition should of course be credited to our office, but really should be credited to Rem, because although I worked on many of the projects exhibited in there, I did not work on this exhibition itself. So while I'm mesmerised and fascinated by the story of the Hitler furniture, I couldn't really tell you.

But I think the beautiful point of it – now that I think of it, and this is my interpretation – is that we propose that we shouldn't necessarily preserve only the 'good' but that we should preserve history, and that history is inevitably a mix of good and bad and therefore, yes, the chairs of Hitler are, you know ... *Hitler*, and Hitler is a symptom of a bad regime, but nevertheless it's a regime that ought to be remembered because it's such a vital part of our history. But that kind of courtesy is totally not extended in the architectural world in the sense that the utopian efforts of the 1960s and the 1970s are now subject to a kind of universal demolition; it's almost as if that period of our history is completely erased as though it never existed and that's the confusion – that's the 'Cronocaos' – that's the confused state of the architectural world that it adds a *moral* dimension to what it preserves, whereas with preservation it's essential to preserve history in all its splendour and in all its misery. But I just made that up on the spot.

RH: Well, let's move onto the Roadmap project then, because that's what you're here to discuss today. It's a big statement from the office in terms of how to engage with sustainability, and one of the interesting ideas in your writing on it is this necessity to *scale up*; that actually architecture as a discipline of buildings is incapable of dealing with the scale of the climate crisis.

RdG: Well, it wasn't always – and that's the weird irony. Relating back to the same period that is now being demolished, architecture was aggressively utopian and also aggressively bold in claiming the scale at which the issue needed to be addressed. It didn't have this voluntary self-confinement to the scale of a building simply because it was their discipline. I mean, there was no inhibition. If anything, with the Roadmap project, we are critiquing the architectural world for forgetting its own tradition in being involved at that scale. In that sense, the Roadmap project is also a deliberate disclaimer of originality, it's a form of remembering. And maybe it's also even a form of preservation, in that it simply highlights a particular architectural period which *now* through the momentum of the climate, through the momentum of energy and sustainability, could have a totally valid ticket to be no longer utopian.

RH: Throughout all this work and this style of thinking there seems to be the presence of Buckminster Fuller, whose projects of the 1960s and 1970s were at the time – as you say – incredibly utopian, but now it

65   Reinier de Graaf & Laura Baird

seems like this 'whole-earth' approach is our only option.

LB: The thing about infrastructure at a large scale, and one of the things our office likes about the work of Fuller, is that it suggests that designers are part of the solution to sustainability, and not just designing a two by two metre green roof. You have to think about infrastructure on a large scale as climate change is inherently a global problem that requires a global solution. As urban planners by training or architects by training, we can kind of assess the territorial claims and spatial implications of this, but also that it is something that needs to be designed in order to be carried out. It's not a political problem – I mean of course politicians need to get involved and policy makers need something to base their decisions and their mandates on – but perhaps that's something that needs to be designed in the end.

EU exhibition tent at Place de Schuman roundabout Brussels, in the colours of AMO's proposal for a new European Union flag.

RdG: AMO have of course done an earlier project on Europe, on Europe as a project, as a political construct, and the relevance of that political construct. The nice thing about the Roadmap energy project is that it gives a very pragmatic reason to do some of the things we suggested, even when it was still only a political project. But of course when those things are political they are by definition difficult and subject to dissent, whereas if they are practical and pragmatic they are much more likely to find consensus.

What's interesting is that the European Union started as the European Union for Coal and Steel, and it had a pragmatic industrial *raison d'être* – which was perhaps used to shield part of their political motives – but nevertheless, consensus was more easily mobilised around a practical issue. And the wonderful thing about the Roadmap energy project is that it has that same potential, but at a much larger scale than the original six member states.

RH: To operate on the scale of the continent seems so far away from the core of architecture, not only in terms of scale, but also conceptually. What motivated you to address climate change directly in this way? Should architects take on this kind of responsibility for issues more broadly?

RdG: It's an interest in planning also; we've found that much of the thinking we've developed through urban planning could very simply be applied to this issue in quite a wonderful way: to check population density against the presence of energy sources linking them for instance. These are in a way much the same motions that you go through when you plan an extension of a city, or a new city even. Yes it's a much much bigger scale than of course any urban planning exercise, but it doesn't feel unnatural. Well, of course you feel out of your depth because it's monumental, but on a day-to-day basis it doesn't feel like an unnatural thing to be dealing with. I mean, there are other subjects where I have many more inhibitions related to my ignorance than here.

LB: Just feeding off that a bit, of course the world has realised that reducing carbon emissions is a global challenge; a challenge to stop emitting, to become sustainable, to plan renewable energy infrastructure

Reinier de Graaf & Laura Baird

Overleaf: AMO's Fuller-esque Future World Energy Grid.

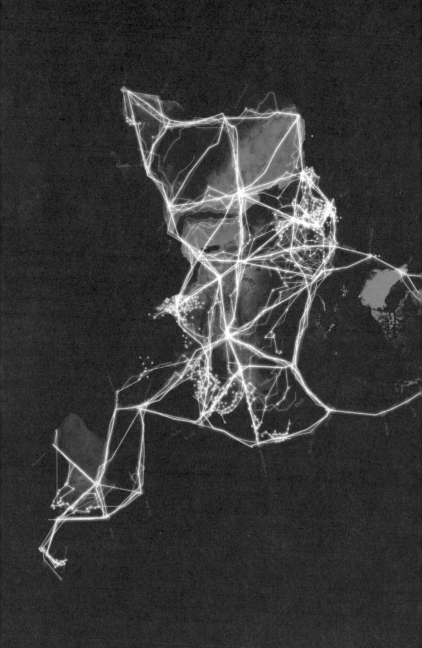

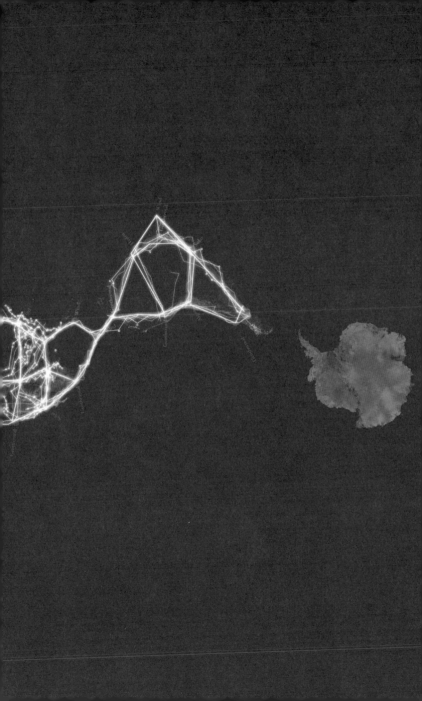

etc. But the global climate summits like Copenhagen or Cancun, where they are trying to solve these challenges on a world scale, continue to fail. So you can plan any number of summits and you're going to get no result. But what we try to show through our work is that if you plan something *physical,* it's not that we intend to see it built exactly the way that we've planned it, but it's to show a feasible proposal for something that *could* happen that offers a potential solution to challenges that that aren't currently being solved, even though they are being addressed at that scale already, just not in the realm of design.

RdG: The trouble with dealing in particularly technical issues – and we've had it before planning hospitals or planning airports – is that the responses are so overwhelmingly dominated by technical and specialist knowledge, that a certain level of conceptual overview, even a certain level of common sense, is missing. There may be completely logical things nearby which you missed because you're looking at a footnote under a microscope. In that sense even a relative ignorance on the technical matters can be an advantage if you are in the position to make a synthesis.

LB: It makes it accessible. I mean the fact that we're, let's say, relatively *naïve* compared to the technical experts, we have to synthesise the material and present it in a way that we can understand it first, and then if we can understand it others can hopefully understand it as well. By approaching it from first principles, we can relearn the problem as a way of coming up with our own solution.

RH: Just to finish up then, what's up the status of the project? What has been the response from the policy makers? What has been the response from the European Union?

LB: The status is good: we've presented to a number of ministers, we had a series of launches across the countries of the EU 27, and it will be taken up at the European Commission council meeting in October. In particular the Minister for Energy and the Environment is quite enthusiastic, and in an ideal world some of the principles of the Roadmap would be incorporated into Europe's energy policy in the coming years. But I think with respect to our ambitions for the project, we've used it as a springboard within our own office to really delve into other projects of multiple scales from very very controlled technical design proposals to proposals on the scale of the entire world. So there are exciting things to come.

Reinier de Graaf & Laura Baird

THE DOUBLE AGENT

Mel Dodd

muf_aus

What constitutes architecture is a deceptively thorny question. We are surrounded by buildings, yet few of these will find their way into architectural journals, and in the case of houses, few are even designed by architects. Historian Nikolaus Pevsner attempted to lay this matter to rest by famously declaring that 'a bicycle shed is a building; Lincoln Cathedral is a piece of architecture'. Alone, this distinction seems clear, but where is the line between these two typologies? And besides, the international competition held by London's Architecture Foundation early in 2011 to 'design a bike shed' surely rebukes Pevsner's easy classification altogether. So if a bicycle shed can be architecture, then why not a bench?

The Diorama Bench (2008, ongoing) by Melbourne-based architect Mel Dodd stands as a further challenge to the limitations of what constitutes architecture. Conceived for the Western Reserve of Hastings in Victoria, Diorama Bench captures a 'microcosmic representation of scenes from the everyday life of local children in

Dodd's Diorama Bench speculates on the values of 'un-designed space, feral land and the rural urban fringe'.

Mel Dodd

peripheral and feral ground', in the form of tiny models built into the bench itself, and acts as a venue for further engagements with the young people and adult residents of the area. Forming part of a larger design framework titled Do-It-Yourself-Park, this humble bench illustrates the role that a tiny physical structure can play in facilitating a larger civic agenda, one that Dodd would undoubtedly consider 'architectural'.

Dodd, who is a partner of the UK-based, socially engaged art-architecture collective muf, relocated to Melbourne in 2004 where she established muf_aus, a satellite branch that is at once conceptually related and autonomous. Dodd is now also program director of the architecture school at RMIT University, where she recently completed her PhD, titled 'Between the Lived and the Built', which reflects on her project work spanning the public realm, social policy, education, urban renewal, participatory design and cultural strategies.

A key contribution of Dodd's thesis is the identification of the various roles and persona she adopts when undertaking these projects, including 'the local', 'the double agent', 'the educator', 'the artist', and 'the policy maker'. Intentionally diverse and unorthodox, as Dodd

The Double Agent

explains, these roles 'do not take on the conventional characteristics of the architect as a professional responsible for designing buildings', but instead explore strategies beyond building.

The ability to inhabit these different personas is itself a characteristic of a 'double agent', who infiltrates territories or organisations foreign to one's own in order to collect intelligence, while actually serving the needs of that foreign organisation. By leaving the traditionally conceived role of the architect behind and embedding within a community, Dodd is able to better understand and serve their needs, even if they're as humble as a bench.

Conducted 30th November 2011 over Skype between Amsterdam and Melbourne.

Rory Hyde: I thought we could start with this quote from *The Architects' Journal* which you refer to in your PhD: 'The real test will only come when muf are able to realise a significant building'. It seems to perfectly capture the pervasive idea of what constitutes 'real' architecture. How might you counter that claim? And if architecture is more than just building, what is the neglected terrain that you are interested in?

> Mel Dodd: We once had an anonymous and quite nasty fax come through that sarcastically referred to our 'magnificent achievements' – 'muf designs park bench'. We always laughed hilariously at it, because it really missed the point, as though there was only one objective in doing architecture. I don't think we hold

Mel Dodd

Using 19th-century architectural salvage, The Folly by muf for Barking Town Square recovers the lost historical fabric of the town centre.

any antithetical views about buildings – that's the object in some ways – but mainly our work has been interested in the fringes where, as Cedric Price would say, 'the answer may not be a building'. I would go further – there may not be an answer.

For me, muf as a collection of practitioners has always been about learning from the context of working with artists and understanding that in art practice, especially in socially engaged art practice, there is no objective, in a way. There is an objective to make something, but that something might not be physical; it could be a moment, an event, a video or whatever. I do think that's the most critical thing, that the conventional understanding that architects only design buildings can be dissolved if you start to work outside your own discipline. That's not to say buildings aren't interesting, but it's the edges between the two.

RH: This idea of the edge is a central theme of your thesis, what you call the zone 'between the lived and the built'. You state this 'is the domain that presents the architect with a great deal of difficulty', and yet to many architects this space is probably invisible, or it is at least accepted that there's an inevitable break between what is designed and how it is inhabited. How do you conceive of this space, and why is it difficult?

> MD: It hinges on the presumption that the role of the architect is to design a building, and when the work is finished, you leave and the building then goes into a second stage of occupation. This idea that you're somehow an expert because you design buildings always makes me feel a bit uncomfortable. It's frustrating that the discipline of architecture is poorly understood; it is both culturally critical and pervasive, but at the same time as an architect you get pigeonholed into the production of buildings alone. So there's an idea that maybe you can extend your role beyond the final completion – maybe there's an overlap, and maybe you're interested in the way people occupy buildings, and the way you might make very small changes to intercede in those occupations. I just enjoy not having an explicit boundary of what is considered architecture.

RH: I'm interested in this suspicion you might have of the 'expert', that somehow the privileged perspective of the architect separates us from reality. This points to one of the roles you foreground in your work, that of 'the local', where the architect adopts the position of a user. It seems to be an explicit challenge to our specialised knowledge, but how can we actually occupy that role in a real sense? Do we need to unlearn what we know? And doesn't our training offer us a constructive perspective and a useful set of skills?

> MD: I think that's right, it's important to maintain an understanding of our own extra knowledge. By becoming a local, it's not that we somehow have to

hand over our expertise to local people, which is the participatory planning model where you all sit around a table with the butterpaper and say 'you do it'. Rather, we swap places backwards and forwards in a way that both acknowledges some of the things that we have within our training that are special, but also acknowledges what other people have in their knowledge and experience that's special. In that process you thicken up the content.

I've always really loved the idea that the expert might be many people – the architect, the local council, or even the child aged five who has lived in a place all their life – it's an expertise about that place. It's not to say that a five-year-old should design the building, but about somehow allowing that particular point of view to inform you.

I'm always a bit horrified when people misinterpret this type of practice as some sort of participatory 'free-for-all', but it's not that at all, it's much more about saying there's a whole range of contested opinions – I have one, and someone else might have another – and seeing how on earth we can avoid an average design-by-committee scheme, by actually having some sort of collaborative presence, if in a contested way. As the muf book puts it, 'a continual process of give and take, a two-way stretch between the practitioner and interested parties'.

RH: Beyond this community or participatory approach, some of the other roles you identify are far more subversive, in particular the 'double agent'. How does the double agent operate? Is it a sort of guerrilla architect?

MD: The double agent is about understanding that in the realms of architectural commissioning and procurement, architecture struggles when it attempts to be an act of resistance. And yet we are interested in architecture as an act of resistance. So you have to operate in different modes simultaneously in order to get something done. This mode of the double agent allows you to take on a commission with a certain value structure and, at the same time, to work against it; to be an activist as well as an entrepreneur. So you might work on how a project can get funding to become a real thing, but also on how to prevent it from becoming subsumed within the ideological rhetoric of community building or neighbourhood renewal, or social policy outcomes. In that sense, working within these environments, which we mainly have, can get quite unpleasant if you are somehow problem-solving as if complex social and economic disadvantage for example can be solved by architectural interventions. I guess that's where the double agent comes from; it's a useful ambiguity. It taps into this idea that architecture is in a bind between wanting to be socially, politically and culturally relevant, and being totally strung up by the need to deliver outcomes within standard forms of capitalist funding. And you are either on one side of the bind or the other. The double agent is a way that you might be both.

RH: Scale also seems to play an important part in the ability to operate in different modes and to promote a social agenda, which is perhaps much more difficult when you're working on a big building with lots of capital and the sorts of obligations that come with it. Is your focus on the small an intentional limitation, a way to remain focused on people?

MD: I think partly you are right, that I, and muf, choose to operate at a particular scale because it's easier to work ambiguously, and that's more interesting to us. And I do think large-scale practice makes it more and more difficult to entertain some of these other debates. But it's also not about saying 'I don't want to do anything that's bigger than a bench', because the bulk of the work is all about the city: how we live in the city, how we operate within it, and the dilemmas of contested space within the city. It's about saying, 'Well, if you're interested in a very big scale, but you can also see these conflicts, how do you work at a big scale and remain in some way intimate?' It's about a different sort of urban planning. A lot of the projects are about deliberately taking the scale down to where it's about fragments, small things, understanding quite fragile qualities of the city and working on those. Because by understanding what's there, instead of overlaying something else on top of it, you are rather exposing it and bringing it to bear. It's about understanding what city planning could be, if it's not always ideologically motivated around improvement. I think the issue of scale is incredibly interesting.

RH: I agree, scale is often dismissed as an arbitrary limit, but I think we need to be braver in confronting it as a useful idea, because for me it offers the strongest correlation with a whole range of other desirable social effects. But just to shift gears a little, I'm interested in why you came to Australia, because for somebody interested in this type of practice it doesn't seem like there's much going on. The definition of architecture in Australia is almost strictly professional, which is largely the reason I left!

The Double Agent

MD: The main reason is the accident of life. Although I spent a good part of my childhood in Australia, I wouldn't have known without coming to Melbourne as an architect and academic, that my form of practice, a kind of acupuncture or adjustment, as nurtured in England and Europe, doesn't happen so much here. The cities are less established, with fewer constraints on what you can do and quite a lot of space for new architecture. Young, cutting-edge architects in Australia face a totally different challenge, probably one that is more about form making. I didn't quite work that one out…

When I left the UK in 2004, I began to feel that the whole movement toward working with communities and integrating social policy stuff into projects for the city, which emerged from New Labour, was a new orthodoxy. I was in a department in a university that was entirely about that; bizarrely I felt like it was very mainstream. And actually, coming to Melbourne has been really helpful to understand and reflect on a broader context of socially engaged architecture, and, combined with this, discover evidence of some people's resistance to it. This experience has taught me that it can be interpreted as a sort of paternalistic, ideological approach, that in working in the social and political realm you therefore have some belief you are going to change things, that you can ameliorate situations. And that this might be problematic.

RH: Well that is interesting; perhaps I mistakenly thought that was true! Whether it's perceived as being paternalistic or not, surely you are interested in measurable change, in being ameliorative, and not just exercising the image of change?

Mel Dodd

MD: I agree with you, I've never had a problem with the fact that the work you do might be trying to ameliorate a situation. It's just that I've become sensitised to this knotty, slightly self-conscious view, which dissects this idea and says 'Ah, but who are you to try and solve my situation? And who are you to say that

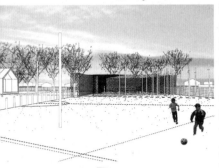

this is wrong?' I think it stems from a worldwide shift in a way, that there's no ideology, there's no meta-theory, and you can't generalise, assume, or overlay ideas about 'improvement' without understanding the context of your own prejudices and experiences. In some ways this is in tune with muf's own practice, which inter-

Multi-Use Games Area for Hastings, a 'sociable cage' allowing multiple occupations of space.

venes as a form of provocation, rather than trying to provide an answer. But you can't say that something you do doesn't have an effect, and that the effect might not be a good one. But I guess I've become hypersensitive to that because of being in a context where some people are resistant to the concept that you can do good with architecture.

RH: It's a strange concept to be resistant to!

MD: Isn't it? It's weird. It seems to emanate from two different trajectories of practice, one that is interested in form-making, pleasure and experience, people who think it's much too complicated so don't even go there, and another set of people who are highly socially and politically self-conscious and interested, but who then think it's too simplistic; that it is beyond the remit of architecture. Whereas to look back at European practice now, there are a lot of practices doing stuff that is marginal and politically motivated, but beyond building if you like, and there's usually no embarrassment in talking about it in that way. Having said all that, I don't know how important these distinctions between Australia, England and anywhere else actually are.

RH: I'm less interested in casting generalisations, but more in the idea that Australia might be changing, which I feel is certainly the case in the last few years. These strict distinctions between one place being open, or not, to different kinds of social spatial practice are becoming blurred.

MD: That's right. I noticed there was a 'Right to the City' symposium for architects earlier in the year, in Sydney. It seemed to collect an interesting set of people; I was quite reassured by that in a way.

Of course what's disappointing about avoiding a social agenda for architecture – horrifying in a way – is that there's as much disadvantage in Australia as anywhere, it's just hidden. I feel a lot of Australians think this is not relevant to them for some reason. You just need to look at a few outer suburbs or take the train to Frankston [in Melbourne] like I do every day to see this massive inequality. It's our role as cultural activists to behave with that in mind; it's as relevant here as it is in Europe.

RH: Timothy Moore and I interviewed Esther Charlesworth from Architects Without Frontiers about a year ago,[18] and she said that after a decade of working overseas, in Bosnia, Beirut, India and Nepal, she came back to Australia and was shocked to find the same problems, if not worse, happening in a wealthy,

Western democracy. We're certainly not short on terrain to operate in this way.

> MD: Exactly. So this idea that we are squeamish or that it's too paternalistic to go and say that we could do something, seems like a complete loss to me. Like the easy way out of the bind. I run a studio at RMIT that looks at areas of disadvantage, and at social inequity as a spatial condition – but as an agenda for design, I notice it is in the minority.

RH: Actually, [Harvard University professor and former director of Foreign Office Architects] Farshid Moussavi was under fire for suggesting this in a lecture just the other day. She criticised students for going to Haiti or Africa or Vietnam to work on community projects, when there is so much need for it in the US. I think her point is that community or social work shouldn't be a gap year for experience, it should actually just form part of your practice.

> MD: It doesn't have to be framed that you are somehow 'do-gooding'; it can be framed as your actual role, as a duty of care, a custodianship.

THE
HISTORIAN
OF THE
PRESENT

Wouter
Vanstiphout

Crimson

Founded in 1994 by Wouter Vanstiphout and Michelle Provoost, Crimson describe themselves as 'historians of the present', an inherently contradictory statement that nevertheless proves to be surprisingly useful. They deploy the tools of the historian – research, analysis, synthesis – to not only chronicle the past, but also as a practical tool in shaping the future. History is treated as something that can be 're-designed', or 'narrativised'; as Vanstiphout explains, 'once you re-tell the story you have something you can manipulate, it becomes actionable'.

This interest in the active potential of history found its ultimate testing ground when, in 2001, Crimson were invited to compile the bidding documents for the redevelopment of the suburb of Hoogvliet, a predominantly poor neighbourhood on the outskirts of Rotterdam. While Crimson's role began simply as editors, they had a fundamental disagreement with the initial concept of the redevelopment proposal: to demolish all of the social housing and to bring in the 'best architects' to replace it, *tabula rasa*. Crimson argued that they '[did] not think that architecture should play this role, it's not interesting and nobody will be interested', and instead put together its own counter proposal with the politician Felix

Wouter Vanstiphout

Rottenberg, informed by a 'deep comprehension of the area; socially, architecturally and historically'.

Appropriately titled WiMBY! or Welcome into My Backyard, Crimson initiated an intimate process of consultation with the local residents, producing a plan based entirely on the needs and desires of the community, rather than any externally imposed idea of what the place should be. The resulting plan was far cheaper to implement than the originally proposed scheme, so 'it was very easy to win', never mind that it was ideologically opposed to the aims and experience of the development partners...

When it became evident that those tasked with implementing the plan were uncooperative, the Crimson partners simply rolled up their sleeves and took it on themselves. As Vanstiphout describes, 'we had already made the leap from historians to architects, and then we made the leap from architects to developers'. For the past ten years, they have guided this project through every level of decision-making: from finding investors, obtaining planning permits, consulting with the residents, attending meetings to discuss the heating systems, and even coordinating events in the buildings once they were complete.

The Historian of the Present

Despite the exhausting effects of the bureaucracy, politics and tedium of the world of property development, Crimson persevered throughout the process, as it offered them a unique insight into the real forces that shape the city, which, as historians, they could only view from a distance. This experience could then be fed back into their writing work, closing the loop between action and reflection. As Vanstiphout explains, 'in a way that has become our model, the theoretical work is embedded in the practical work, and we do the practical work in order to better do the theoretical work'.

Vanstiphout's recent appointment as Professor of Design and Politics at Delft University of Technology (TU Delft) offers him a platform from which to extend this meta-view of the planning and development world. Through an examination of architecture's changing relationship to politics, power, economics and society, students are prepared to engage these forces of 'dark matter' – as Vanstiphout calls them – in a more relevant and engaging way.

Rory Hyde: As part of your new appointment at TU Delft you presented the lecture series *Blame the Architect?*, examining the 'failure' of urban planning schemes of the post-war period. In particular you researched the riots in the *banlieue* areas of low-income housing on the outskirts of Paris in 2005. What are the lessons architecture students can take away from this? Can we blame the architect?

> Wouter Vanstiphout: Well, with the whole story about the riots, and what I try to give the students there – therapeutically of course – is a kind of sense of deep desperation and self-doubt, but also a sense of how society sometimes looks at architecture. I often think that architects have no idea what they are being accused of; it's like Kafka – they have no idea what the charges actually are, but they are serious.
>
> But the other side of that story is that I really do not know what my clear-cut position on that question would be; can we blame the architect? Can we blame the type of planning, the spatial qualities, or the 'added value' of the architect for at least *part* of the poverty, alienation, frustration, aggression and crime etc. that has become associated with these types of developments?

RH: The most damning evidence which you present against architects' 'innocence' would seem to be this incredible claim that the riots in France *only* occurred in neighbourhoods built in this particular modernist style from this particular period. A hundred percent correlation between burning cars and Corbusian-inspired high rises.

WV: Yes, hundred percent correlation. With one exception – well, it's only an exception in the sense that not *all* high rises had riots. The one city where there was a big ethnic community, big tensions, and a huge concentration of these high rises, there were no problems. Why? Because they were downtown, very close to the centre of the city, interwoven with the social fabric, so they did not feel isolated.

Rioting in the *banlieues* of Paris, 2005.

So there is a kind of tentative conclusion that I am working on: I don't think it is the design or the spatial qualities that we added to these places that are the problem, but that these places are still being seen as 'projects'. What all these areas had in common was that they had been vilified for years already, and all of them had been treated in the press and by everybody as 'failed' pieces of the city. And somehow the dominant rhetoric became that we have to 'solve' them by demolishing them. I think that the demolition plans for these areas are just as *tabula rasa* as the principles on which they were once built. The idea to *demolish* housing projects in order to solve social problems is just as megalomanic as *building* housing projects in order to solve social problems.

So it is not so much Le Corbusier who is to blame, but it is the Le Corbusier in *us* who is to blame. Because if you say that something is a failed city, it means you can also say that something is a successful city, meaning that you speak about cities as business plans. If it's in the red it's a failure, if it's in the black it's good. And this is ridiculous! It's like talking

Wouter Vanstiphout

about people as successes or failures depending on how much money they make – which of course we actually do – but we don't think that it's a good thing.

RH: This reminds me of something you said in your lecture at the Architecture Association:[19] 'if architecture can claim to solve problems, then it's only logical that it can also be blamed'. So you can't have it both ways.

WV: That's right, you can't say 'I can solve problems, but I'm not to blame if I cause a problem', it's impossible. If you can use a knife to cut a steak, you can also use a knife to stab someone. So it's a choice you have to make, and it's a funny philosophical choice that architects have never really made. For example, the whole discussion about Robin Hood Gardens,* where even Zaha Hadid says 'this is important architecture and we have to save it', I find this so puzzling, because all these visionary architects said that the architecture could not be blamed for the problems happening in Robin Hood Gardens. So if architecture cannot be blamed, then it also cannot be thanked. And therefore as an architect you can't claim to create a social transformation in your own architecture.

* Robin Hood Gardens is a brutalist style council housing complex in London, designed by Alison and Peter Smithson in the late 1960s, currently under threat of demolition.

RH: Robin Hood Gardens is an interesting example because the Smithsons' rhetoric was so community-oriented and so utopian, but one which has so radically mismatched the results. So is the lesson then for architects to just be more humble?

WV: I am seriously and deeply ambiguous about this whole question [laughs]. On the one hand, of course architects should be more humble, but on the other hand if they are humble, what good are they?

RH: Do you see your work in Hoogvliet, where you have retained many of the existing so-called 'failed' buildings, added some new small-scale buildings, all determined by an intimate process of local community engagement etc., as humble?

WV: I would not say that was humble, and having done that project I don't think that you can be humble. I think that our project is deeply arrogant – I hope in a good way – in the sense that if you are humble, and if you take this humility to the extreme, it would mean that you would accept everything instead of challenging it. So in Hoogvliet, we would accept that the social segregation was happening and that there was not much you could do about it. When actually we were like schoolteachers, practically slapping them and ferrying them about. We organised an exhibition and we actually went around with buses and knocked on doors to bring them there. Because we knew that in a society in Hoogvliet that people would never go. So we really, literally rounded them up, we *forced* ourselves on these people. Now I'm from Belgian ancestry, and I nearly felt like one of those Catholic missionaries in Congo, forcing my beliefs on the poor natives! So there is no humility.

RH: I'm going to quote your essay from the *Open City* catalogue,[20] where you mention that the status of the architect is now at a high point, Rem, Zaha, Frank and Norman have all become household names, gracing the covers of magazines and flying around the world. But you also see this popularity as having *marginalised* the architect in a way; you say that 'to restore architecture and planning to a position where

　　　Wouter Vanstiphout

it can have a real positive impact on society may even demand destroying the mythology of the architect as visionary'. How do we reconcile this need on the one hand to make big plans, but also not to be so definitive?

> WV: Well, this was written in the wake of the financial crisis, and we made this kind of analogy between how financial products are being created and sold that have lost any connection with real production or a real economy. And in the same way architecture has drifted into the stratosphere, where it's not even simply that *designs* are being produced which have no relationship to actual *buildings*, but it's even that the *buildings* that are being produced have no relationship to actual *needs*. Instead they are being produced for city marketing, or to create objects that investors can speculate in. Even – as you know – some of the buildings in Dubai were standing empty and earning an enormous amount of money; just to rent them out would be a headache, as the rental earnings would be so marginal compared to the speculative earnings.

> Now I think the visionary part of architecture *is* important, I think there *is* a real and important role for visionary architecture, but right now, especially that part of it, is completely bankrupt and empty. When an architect now proposes a speculative or visionary design, it does not have the same meaning as when they did it in the 1970s or the 1930s, it has a completely different role, and I think that now in the current environment it has no positive role.

RH: It's interesting, I often think about this contradiction in the way we talk about vision. Architects still seem unable to confront the 1970s; it's a time when

The Historian of the Present

our best intentions were revealed to also be our biggest failures. And because of that, we're also afraid of never being asked to design on that scale again. So on the one hand, the rhetoric at the moment seems to be 'crisis' – the financial crisis, the environmental crisis, the crisis of social cohesion, the ageing crisis – but then on the other hand, the greatest solution on the table at the moment seems to be *urban farming*. So while the challenges we face are at their most formidable, our response is at its most polite. Do you think that is the legacy of the 1970s playing out? A reaction against that hubris?

> WV: I don't know, maybe this is a more cynical explanation of it, but it seems that the whole idea of the profile of the star architect seems to be shifting from Rem Koolhaas, who is still kind of in the family of Le Corbusier – coolness, shrillness, European-ness, a kind of 'robot man', you know, publishing endlessly, opinionated about everything, but also unapproachable – and it has progressed towards Bono. So there seems to be a new kind of player now. I've seen it teaching in Delft, where if you want to get all the students behind you, you have to do projects in Haiti, or you have to do self-build projects in the slums of Peru, or urban farming. When I taught in Berlin a couple of years ago, I already saw this happening; architects would say 'I am a DJ and we organise parties because that is real architecture'. So that is kind of this legacy of the 1960s, but in a way I find this attitude of the smallness, of the doing-it-yourself-ness not as arrogant but even more *vain* in a way.
>
> So I'm really critical and bordering on the cynical about this current obsession with urban intervention, especially because it's so globalised. I mean these

people, they spend thousands of dollars on flights from Amsterdam to Haiti to work with the people – there's something really *spoilt* about it.

RH: 'Spoilt' is a great word. But I have to admit I've dabbled in this urban intervention myself – although here in Rotterdam, not in Haiti – and it was a great project to do, but I guess the bad taste it left in my mouth was that it was so easy, and yet it got so much attention. We didn't go through any of the nightmares that you did in Hoogvliet, we didn't apply for any permissions. We took some great photos, gave away some free beer and got on all the design blogs. And I feel like that is what urban intervention is plugging into, rather than some deeper desire to fix the city, because if that's what you really wanted to do then you would think on a much larger scale.

WV: And that brings us to the real design as politics question. If you really want to change the city, or want a real struggle, a real fight, then it would require re-engaging with things like public planning for example, or re-engaging with government, or re-engaging with large-scale institutionalised developers. I think that's where the real struggles lie, that we re-engage with these structures and these institutions, this horribly complex *dark matter*. That's where it becomes really interesting.

For example now for the Rotterdam Biennale, with my chair at Delft, we are looking at two cities – one in the Netherlands, and one in Brazil – which want to extend huge highways. In both places you can see that all the architects think it's a bad idea, the local government thinks it's a bad idea too, but the state government thinks they have to do it. Left-wing people are against it, right-wing people are for it. So the interesting thing is to understand that it's really a political issue – highways somehow are right wing, and houses are somehow left wing – and it really works like that! You see it even in the Netherlands, the capital of consensus, this polarisation in politics cuts straight down the middle.

One of the challenges that we have put to ourselves is to ask 'Does architecture have the power to propose a highway that would even make the left-wing parties happy?' And you will not do that by making a compromise. It's an experiment, I'm not saying I believe in that kind of thing, but I do believe that architecture and design as a combination of pure speculation, rhetorical poetics and technical capacity could play a role in politics. It could reshape certain discussions and therefore create its own inevitability.

RH: Yes, I've always thought that the role and the strength of architecture in these debates which become so political is to provide an alternative in order to open up the debate. When there's just that one design on the table, and one side is yelling 'No' and the other side is yelling 'Yes' at exactly the same level, you're stuck. But if you can produce this thing which seems to appease both parties, then you can come back to the table.

WV: Exactly, and I think there is a kind of potential for visionaries in that attitude toward design.

RH: Aside from highways, have you found that actual buildings can be so politically divisive?

WV: If it is true, as in Rotterdam for example, that the minaret of a mosque can be the focus of such a huge political effort to ban them, then the way that buildings *look* does have a political relevance. If people

Wouter Vanstiphout

FAT Architects' Heerlijkheid building, part of Crimson's masterplan for Hoogvliet, 2008.

look at minarets in a political way, just as they look at the absence of minarets in a political way, then they look in a political way.

When we were developing the design of the Heerlijkheid in Hoogvliet, this is something we were explicitly researching, which is also the reason that we worked with FAT Architects, to explore the capacity of a narrative architecture. An architecture that can express through ornament the history, the values, the proposed values of a specific place. Which in Hoogvliet is this strange combination of the rustic, the pastoral, the industrial and the suburban; the building is loaded with references, and even the golden porchway could be seen as a gas explosion or as some trees.

I also think there is a connection between the high rises in Paris burning up and the way that they look. But the connection is probably the other way around; somehow these same images have gone from representing a *promise* to representing *desperation*. But it's the same image. And I think it is the same with minarets. If we go to Istanbul we see the minaret as part of a tradition, a history, a kind of 'orientalist joy'. And yet maybe even the same people who love them in Istanbul hate them here. So I think there is a real relationship between the aesthetics of architecture and politics, but it's also a relationship that can suddenly switch. So the joyous effect of brutal concrete can flip into blood.

RH: I recently watched a documentary called *The Pruitt-Igoe Myth*,[21] which has interviews with the former residents of this 'failed' housing project who describe the joy of having their own room for the first time in their lives; they never dreamed they would ever live in a bright, new, modern building like it. It initially fulfilled all the utopian claims made for it by the architects. The film then goes to pains to illustrate how the architecture was only one of so many other external causes that led to its transformation into a living hell. But the buildings of course get the blame.

Pruitt-Igoe housing estate in St. Louis, Missouri, shortly after its completion in 1955.

WV: And in a way it's also understandable that the buildings get the blame, because they are the things you can most easily change. Some of the other factors are so deeply complex that you cannot change them.

Another thing we discovered through our research is this kind of controversial idea that democracy and equality is bad for communal housing, because people are relegated there. Whereas at the complete other end of the spectrum, we discovered in cities like Kabul and Tehran, where you have these repressive regimes and repressive religious cultures, that it was the high rises where the secular middle classes *wanted* to live, because there it was exactly the kind of non-social, anonymous, monotonous, alienating qualities of the high rise that created freedom. If they would live in this wonderful souk of inner courtyards

Wouter Vanstiphout

etc., they would be constantly watched over; the whole social fabric would be so dense that they couldn't be anything else. Imagine being a lesbian schoolteacher in the souks of Kabul, the architecture then becomes a form of repression. Whereas the high rises, exactly for the reason that they become a problem in a democratic society, are a kind of solution.

RH: It sounds like such a direct expression of this link between design and politics. The design stays the same, but when you change the politics, you get a completely different result.

WV: Exactly, and that's exactly the point. So I don't think architects have to shed their visionary status, their 'good' arrogance, or their speculative powers, if only they would realise that things are contextual! Acknowledge the fact that the deepest meaning in what they do is directly related to the context in which they do it.

You can draw two lessons from this; either you say 'It's all random, it's all context, you can't do anything', and you're a slave to context. Which for an architect is a death sentence, it's very depressing. Whatever you do is irrelevant; it's all determined by external factors. But you can also draw another lesson – and I hope that this is the real lesson – which is that something that doesn't work here does work there, and there are real reasons for this. So there are ways to really use architecture to change, to give a real alternative, to have a real effect, to be visionary.

Right now the idea to build a high-rise complex in the middle of Tehran would be a visionary thing, and if you would do it it would work fantastically and you would be the world's biggest hero and rightly so.

But then if suddenly Iran gets democracy, it might turn into Pruitt-Igoe!

Wouter Vanstiphout

THE
URBAN
ACTIVIST

Camila
Bustamante

The ability to shape the urban environment is often assumed to be the exclusive preserve of trained architects and urbanists; with years of specialist education and certificates of professional accreditation, these corridors of power are well defended from the public at large.

While the public do shape the environment in various small ways – by creating signage, planting gardens, or simply by occupying space – 'ordinary' citizens are at a disadvantage when it comes to influencing the larger forces of urban strategy, zoning regulations or infrastructure, decisions which are largely handled in a top-down manner at a municipal level.

This exclusivity is being increasingly challenged however, by an emergent force of urban activists, deploying the tactics of public intervention to have their voices heard. This sentiment is captured by David Harvey in the essay 'Right to the City', which calls for the democratisation of the power to shape the urban experience, and further explored by the exhibition 'Actions: What You Can Do With the City', which presented 99 'actions' for intervening in public space, ranging from guerrilla interventions to playful activities.[22, 23] By using strategies outside of those normally taught in the faculties of architecture or

Camila Bustamante

engineering, urban activists are able to reclaim some of the ground lost to professional exceptionalism and collectively shape a more just and social city.

The label 'activist' is not one that Camila Bustamante wears comfortably however. Neither outspoken nor rebellious in character, she is nevertheless motivated by an empathic awareness of the inequalities present in our urban environments. Trained as a graphic designer, Bustamante doesn't use this as an excuse to retreat to the safe confines of the printed page, but instead deploys her skill for communication to address the larger issues of human rights and democracy. Using the familiar and innocuous language of street signage and tourist guides, Bustamante draws attention to complex political and social injustices in a way that is both optimistic and subversive.

Her project Lima 2427, discussed in this interview, used only the lightweight media of stickers and posters to create a ripple of public awareness and political accountability that would ultimately influence the most substantial and concrete outcome: the resurrection of Lima's elevated metro lines, decades after construction had been suspended.

Lima 2427 and Bustamante's subsequent project Todos Somos Dateros ('We Are All Data Providers') has earned this gentle agitator attention from such high-profile institutions as the World Bank, where she and her partners were invited to present in early 2011.

Bustamante applying a sticker indicating a proposed metro stop and the year of its projected completion.

Although not an architect, Bustamante is included here to illustrate that when objectives are reframed to target a specific issue, even the most minimal of interventions can lead to immense results. As architects, we could stand to learn from this, by expanding our repertoire to include strategies of public awareness as a tool to enact change. It may not make us rich, but we might make the lives of others richer in the end.

Conducted 1st April 2011 at Rory's studio in Amsterdam.

Rory Hyde: Let's start at the top. I remember you told me you worked with some NGOs in Lima as a designer?

Camila Bustamante: Yes, in Peru there are a lot of NGOs, because NGOs do the work the government doesn't do, although it is responsible. While I was studying I saw the approach of the NGOs to design, and their strategies for dealing with the people, and it was very poor. I studied mass communication for development, but also took some design subjects in parallel in the art faculty. I had worked a lot with the NGOs so I was always familiar with women's rights and human rights issues, so I was able to combine these interests as a designer.

And then after five years, with all this non-commercial experience, I went into a graphic design studio for some 'real' work experience, yearbooks, infographics and more commercial work. And after that I thought 'OK, I need a masters', and so I came to the Netherlands to study at the Sandberg. My dream was to do something with Lima's multi-cultural identity, its diversity and colonial history. But then the thing that caught my attention the most here was the public transport. Amsterdam is like *heaven* compared to Lima. Not only is the transport a public service, but everybody has the same rights. Transportation is a very good layer to view how a country deals with democracy, human rights, and the equality of people.

RH: In the sense of their access to public transport? Because all the neighbourhoods are equally connected?

CB: Yes, connected, and it's a service for everybody and it's affordable. Lima has not been planned properly, and as a consequence of all the migration from the countryside, it's a very dispersed city. I read that the poorest people spend an average of forty-five percent of their income on transportation and half their time in transit. This is terrible. Access to transport is really a human rights issue. Although with Lima 2427 I consciously chose not to mention equity, democracy, human rights...

The Urban Activist

RH: But underneath it's a very political project. What is the story behind it?

CB: Well, in 1986, Peru's president Alan García announced the project for the *Tren Electrico,* or 'electric train'. They began construction but by the end of García's term the country was bankrupt, with only ten kilometres of track completed and another two long avenues of just columns. When I was growing up, I was used to seeing these columns close to where I lived. It's funny because the mayor of the city turned them into paintings – horrible paintings – but in a way, you get used to these columns.

RH: So the section of the track they built actually works? There's a train that goes back and forth?

CB: You know what's funny: it goes back and forth once a week for maintenance, there's a guy who runs it in case they build the rest. After 1990 some mayors of the city, or even the new President, would open one station as a statement and have a massive wedding in the station, seriously! So once in a while they do an opening and photos, and make a news report. But in daily life people don't really think about the metro or what it was meant to be, they don't even know what the total plan is.

I only discovered the plan when I was here in Amsterdam doing some research; there was a report commissioned in 2001 by the Japanese International Corporation, a train company, which claimed that the first two lines would be complete by 2015. I was completely surprised. But I thought it would never be done, because in twenty years we only have ten kilometres. So I thought, 'Why not do it the other way around, and measure time with distance?' At the

Camila Bustamante

current rate of construction we calculated the entire metro would be complete in the year 2427.

It was a very simple campaign, just some stickers and posters saying '2427: Better late than never, the train is coming!' with a map of where the stations are and when they would open. Design in this case really helped me to legitimise this imaginative scenario. I tried to be as official as possible, to make it look like a real map, to play with the idea of a future that never happened. It got a lot of attention from the media, and was also on TV, which was huge for me.

Map of Lima's proposed metro network redrawn by Bustamante to include the projected dates of completion based on rate of construction.

RH: I know the project is not about politics and you don't mention it explicitly, but I think it's important to discuss because for you, and perhaps for people from Lima, the politics is implicit...

CB: Yes, I don't really talk about it that way because I was also a little scared. Once you do a project with the metro, it's immediately related to President García, especially as he is now back in power again twenty years later. Which is more or less why I chose the map and the signage as a platform. I wanted to work with an established set of 'neutral' symbols, to try to address this issue in a more pragmatic and tangible way. So I tried to be careful to mention this as something neutral. Because, yes, I was also scared.

RH: What would you have been scared of?

CB: What we did was very small, but you never know what can happen. It's quite provocative and critical of the government and the corruption surrounding the contracts for the metro. I remember when I was sticking a poster up somewhere, one guy said 'Watch out what you are doing'. I don't think I would have done it if I was staying in Lima; two days later I was back here in Amsterdam. I didn't plan it like that, maybe it was more of an intuitive strategy to just run away, to feel safe.

RH: Did the media attention have any effect? Did the government respond?

CB: No, but there were some reports and articles, putting this issue back in people's minds again. There was no official response from the minister of transport, but maybe that's better. And besides, I wasn't in Lima anymore. It would have been nice to talk with them, to ask 'What do you think about this?', but it didn't happen. The funny thing was, I did this in September 2009 and at the end of November the President announced the train project will be revived.

I saw a couple of articles mentioning my name, they said 'Camila should estimate the time again, because this time the train will be finished'. But the problem was they only announced the construction of one line, no one talks about the entire plan.

Citizens of Lima discussing their forthcoming metro.

RH: And when do they propose to finish it?

CB: In July 2011, because the President's term is up then. So they are building it now and very quickly. I was in Peru in January and in July. Now it's about finished. They are testing the trains.

RH: I think your project has something to do with this...

CB: I hope so, I hope that it had an effect. But in a way it had to be done, García had to repair his legacy.

RH: It shows how powerful design can be. Your intervention was so tiny, so simple, just one person making some flyers and some stickers, but the total effect is massive: they're out there building the metro. Whether that has anything explicitly to do with you or not, the fact that you influenced the discussion in the media and brought this back into people's minds, shows the power of your very strategic intervention.

CB: Yes, but now I'm trying something different, with a longer-term approach. I think it's very easy to criticise and get attention, but it's much more difficult to do something constructive.

Lima metro under construction.

The Urban Activist

THE CONTRACT UAL INNOVATOR

Steve Ashton ARM

Discussions of new models of architectural practice inevitably lead to the same complaint: we can't change the way we practise unless we can change the contracts. Even a relatively small project, such as a house, involves legal and contractual agreements between the architect, client, builder and various consultants, which appear to be a complex interlocking puzzle of risk avoidance and liability. This is largely accepted as a definitive condition, an unbreachable obstacle that is too embedded in our working procedures and too far outside our expertise to amend. But for a profession explicitly directed to enacting change, why don't architects treat their contractual agreements as another opportunity for design?

'I don't think they try', says Steve Ashton, founding director of Melbourne-based architects Ashton Raggatt McDougall (ARM) and an expert in alternative contract management and procurement methods. Ashton is the least visible of the ARM directors – his colleagues Howard Raggatt and Ian McDougall have the public profiles as designers – but it is arguably his expertise in the less glamorous art of drafting project frameworks and agreements that enables the practice to deliver their highly conceptual and experimental brand of architecture on time and on budget.

ARM's oeuvre is a catalogue of audacity, quotation, criticality and even controversy. The iconic elevation of Robert Venturi's mother's house (1964) is deformed by moving it on a photocopier and then translated directly into brick to form the facade of the Kronborg Clinic (1993), a small medical centre in the Melbourne suburb of Footscray. Their National Museum of Australia in Canberra famously reproduces the fractured zig-zag plan of Daniel Liebeskind's Jewish Museum in Berlin as the gallery for first Australians, drawing an explicit parallel between the holocaust and the mistreatment of Aboriginals by previous generations. Their recent Melbourne Theatre Company is wrapped in an elaborate web of white tubing, creating distortions and false perspectives, and blurring the building's envelope.

This highly lyrical use of form leaves you either engaged or offended, but never indifferent. ARM takes risks, so it is all the more impressive that they also stand as a model of professionalism and good practice, defying the commonplace opposition between the two. Indeed, in many ways it is Ashton's focus on the back end of the architectural process as a subject of design that has enabled ARM to transform their experiments on the edge of architecture into highly resolved and sustainable contributions to the built environment.

In this interview, Ashton discusses the distinct platforms of engagement and collaboration behind some of ARM's largest and most prestigious projects, including the Victorian Desalination Plant, currently under construction, and the Melbourne Theatre Company and Recital Centre, winner of the 2008 Australian Institute of Architects Victorian Architecture Medal.

Conducted 19th April 2011 at the offices of ARM in Melbourne.

Rory Hyde: We hear a lot of complaints from architects regarding the working systems and regulations we've inherited. The legal framework in the background of a building project seem so embedded in how we are paid, in how we respond to a project brief, that it's become an unassailable barrier. I'm keen to explore the idea that you can treat this contractual aspect of architecture as something that needs to be designed just as much as the building.

Steve Ashton: Well, a contract is just an agreement between two parties – at heart it's no more complicated than that. The way you make a contract can create certain kinds of behaviours. So if a contract is pushing you toward an outcome you don't want then you should redesign your contract, or tear it up, because that's just poor design. It's pretty simple. Overriding that is the fact that if you've got the right people on the job, actually the contract doesn't matter that much.

RH: Yes, you need a level of implicit trust for any project to run smoothly.

SA: Exactly. If you've got the right people working together in the right arrangement, you hear people say 'The contract stayed in the drawer, we never read it' – so all that angst, energy and money that went into drafting the contract was a waste of time, because it comes down to the people anyway. I'm happy to argue anytime and anywhere that the most effort that should be put into the project is in selecting the people. The real issue is having the project framework set up properly, and by framework I don't mean contract – I mean is it clear what people want to achieve? Can they afford what they want to achieve? Is the timeline realistic? Those are the *real* guts of a project.

RH: This is an aspect of architecture that's rarely discussed, and yet can have a huge impact on the success of a project.

SA: That's right, the project framework can kill a project, or can lead to a magnificent outcome. If the framework is wrong, badly considered or working against the aims of the project, then it requires an extraordinary effort from the individuals involved to overcome that in order to get a good result; and you would think, 'Well, why would you do that?' It's all just a means to an end, it's so you don't have a miserable life.

RH: Do you think it's more important for the work you do at ARM, compared to other practices? I'm imagining the moment you present the renderings to a client – that moment of shock where they're not even sure what they are looking at, whether it could be built, or brought in on time or on budget. How is the project framework important to your practice specifically? Could you do the work you do without this incredible rigour in the background? I'm thinking of John McArthur's comment in a review of the National Museum of Australia[24] where he says 'those who think of architecture as an elegant ordering of conditions and requirements, will find the NMA wilfully perverse, because of the fact that a simple, efficient and well-considered building is largely invisible under a delirious elaboration of the building's own conceptual system'. This seems to capture this schizophrenia in your work: on the one hand it's making these big gestures, and yet on the other it's very conscious that if it leaks the whole idea is undone.

National Museum of Australia, Canberra. ARM's most lyrical and controversial project includes the iconic plan of Liebeskind's Jewish Museum in Berlin.

SA: That's true, but I wouldn't call it schizophrenia, they're all just givens. Does it have to stand up, does it have to work, does it have to be weather-tight, does it have to be built on time and for a certain amount of money? Of course it does, or else it wouldn't happen. That's just the normal work of a competent architect. You must do all those things, then you have to be better than that – hopefully – and surprise and delight and amaze in the reinterpretation of the client's brief.

When we present our work in other cities, one of the most astonishing questions we get is 'How do you get away with it?' And we reply, 'What do you mean? Get away with what?' The implication is that somehow we've hoodwinked the clients, that they didn't know what they were getting, and we somehow slipped the design through the backdoor. All we've done is exactly what we're meant to do: listened to the client, understood the brief, debated the brief with them, worked out a range of responses, decided on the best direction, developed that direction, and told them the stories. And if they like the stories, then they're on board. And the questions, 'Is it on budget? Is it on time?' Well, yes, of course. I mean, who would bother presenting a project to a client that wouldn't or at least couldn't be?

RH: I'm interested in the role of the architect at this moment in time. Where do we sit in the food chain? The idea that we can be the real project leaders, sitting at the top of the pyramid controlling everybody else, has shifted as projects become more complex – now we're a consultant among many.

SA: That's exactly right. There's still a rump of the profession that believes that the architect is king and is directing everyone else on the project. But that idea went, I don't know how many years ago. It's not relevant anymore apart from on very small projects. For example,

Victorian Desalination Project, a massive infrastructure project almost entirely camouflaged by landscape.

The Contractual Innovator

we're working on the Victorian Desalination Project, a three and a half billion dollar commitment of capital, with four hundred fifty engineers in the project office. Do you think the architect is wandering around asking 'What are you drawing that line over there for?' It's a fantasy.

In that job there is an important role for the architect – together with the landscape architects we set up the master planning for the project, the whole conceptual idea for the way things were to be organised on the site. It's our role to embed that thinking into the project and the project leaders at an early stage. We had twenty-five senior engineers and managers in a room together talking about Aquarius the water carrier and land art, but they all got it. It's not just whimsy or artistic puff, it's a real set of ideas, about respecting those ideas, and realising them to the degree we can afford to realise them. But I don't want you to think it's some kind of bed of roses; you have to do a lot of fighting.

RH: How much influence do you have in that situation? It sounds like an extreme example.

SA: Well, yes, it probably is. We were ten architects among four hundred fifty engineers. It was a very technical project, but we had a reasonable amount of influence. With any big complicated project, your design framework has to be very tough and can't rely on tiny little details – it has to be much more robust than that. It's going to have its arms and legs chopped off and it's going to take a few bullets along the way but it's still got to be able to survive; that's just life in the big world.

RH: What about a more cultural project? Something that's really detail-focused, the Melbourne Theatre

Steve Ashton

Company and Melbourne Recital Centre (MTC/MRC) for instance?

Melbourne Theatre Company and Melbourne Recital Centre.

SA: Well, that was quite different. The MTC/MRC was actually a carefully structured design and construct contract, to which most people would say 'What an appalling way to manage a project'. But it was an idea of the client – which we fully supported – and it was a bloody good idea. Importantly, it started with a very detailed process to ensure we selected the right company to manage the job. The client, Major Projects Victoria, came up with their own list of qualified contractors, and they shortlisted five from those who expressed interest. Those five were then invited to make a detailed submission with the focus on the people who would actually be doing the project and their experience, an indication of the cost of their preliminaries, overheads and profit, plus any other innovations they could bring to the table. This is followed by an interview, with the architects on the other side of the table sitting next to the clients.

Through this process it's surprisingly obvious who are the best people, and they're invited to proceed to another stage. They're then given three months, with full access to work with the drawings and the consultants to submit a guaranteed maximum price for the project, so they end up with a really clear understanding of the project, where all the risks are, the thought processes, so they know exactly what they're getting into. From this we select one contractor who takes responsibility for the design team. Now a lot of senior people in the profession will say 'Shock, horror, you are the servant of the builder', but it's not really like that. You've helped choose them, so you know you haven't got a tosser for a builder, you've got a professional operator who really wants to do the job. So they're not going to treat you like a servant, it's naive to think that.

And I reckon the MTC/MRC is one of the best built public buildings in Australia for a long time. Look at the quality of the build. It's fantastic. We've obviously played a role in that, but so did they. We got the right people. And did we ever look at the contract? No. There's nothing to look at, we just focused on doing the project. We're not lawyers, we're just architects. What we know how to do is really good buildings, and that's what we should do.

RH: One of the other discussions I've had around this topic is that as project managers encroach into the territory that architects once held, the responsibility for the quality of the outcome is no longer there. Project managers are less interested in the design than the architect; it's not their baby. Can those two ideas co-exist?

SA: Yes, of course they can, but it relies on the project manager being professional and competent. Which means adding value to the project. You don't have to be afraid of professional project managers; some people hate them, and it's because there are some really bad project managers. There are some that do nothing, who just pass paper around and make sure someone else gets the blame for everything; well, that's just useless, it's worse than useless actually.

I think the broad trend that you've outlined is no more than what is happening in every walk of life, which is that things are becoming more complicated, and as they get more complicated it is inevitable that the roles will become more specialised. I'll give you a good example: the house I live in was designed by Don Hendry Fulton in 1957. I've got the file: it's got five A2 drawings, no planning permit required, two or three letters from the builder asking for tiny variations, and one letter from the council.

RH: The golden days! I saw the same with the plans for Harry Seidler's mother's house. It was literally just two A0 sheets, plans and elevations on one, details on the other, and that was it, a modern masterpiece.

SA: And just quietly, the architect got eleven percent for that, so no wonder they used to do all right. If we did the same job now, we'd have forty drawings, it would probably take a year to get a planning permit, five lever-arch folders full of correspondence… The specification for this job was twenty double-spaced single-sided pages, you could read it in twenty minutes during your lunch break. It would take a week to read one now. It just shows you what's happened to the world; but there's no point moaning about it, you just have to get on with it. Architects had a broader scope before, but I think it's entirely reasonable that you need a broader team of professional people now to do that today. I think it's still the architect's responsibility to integrate all of the design services together, that's what we do best, and that's what we understand better than anyone else. It's our job to co-ordinate the engineering, the landscape, the graphic design, and the urban design; I think we do that well, that is one of our core competencies.

RH: The other thing you bring up is money. Many architects complain that the core competencies of architecture have been eroded by other consultancies moving in, and that's lessened our slice of the pie, and it's become increasingly difficult to make any money doing what we do.

SA: Well, I just don't agree with that, it's just defeatist thinking – a lack of nerve or something. It actually goes back to procurement. It's relatively easy to tell, when you first come across a project, whether it's one you can make any money on or not. For example, some local governments are notorious for running an architect selection process exactly like they run a process for buying stationery: on price. And if architects are desperate for work they will give a really low price, and they will do what they have to do to survive with their low price. Now, there's not a lot of scope for variation in an architectural contract so you have to cut something. You can't really cut construction documents, because if you do, you get sued. You'll lose your shirt. But you can cut design, because most clients can't tell whether you've cut design or not. And that makes the construction documents that much easier too. So, you can see that this procurement process inevitably leads to poor design outcomes, without an unreasonable effort on the architect's part.

So, as an architect, if you want to do high-quality work and to get paid, don't enter that kind of process. Just don't do it. It can't be done. That takes a bit of nerve sometimes, because your staff expect you to pay them every fortnight, but there's no point in taking on work like that. It's a waste of your life. The more architects that get more discerning and tougher about those sorts of decisions, the better off all architects will be.

Steve Ashton

THE NEAR FUTURE INVENTOR

Matt Webb

BERG

The 21st century was seen as a mythical time of invention and technology in the eyes of the science fiction authors and artists of the 1960s space age: a *Jetsons* world of flying cars and intelligent robot servants, hoverboards and extreme fashion. Looking back from today, we've come to ask 'Where's my jetpack?' – shorthand for the dissatisfaction with the gadgets that the future has wrought; all we have are smartphones.

On first glance, the present has clearly not met the expectations of the past. But of course it's not the smartphone itself which is special, it's the spectacularly complex network of machines and systems that support its existence: a teeming ecosystem of data centres and transmission towers, algorithms and artificial intelligence, that have radically reshaped our experience of time, space and social life. These magical portals have become extensions of ourselves, used to keep us com-

Touch Project investigates the physical space of RFID technology.

pany or incite revolution. Our existence is increasingly predicated on both the physical space of cities, objects and people, and the invisible Hertzian space of electromagnetic waves, wifi and RFID. It is at this junction that the London-based design studio BERG operates.

Led by Jack Schulze, Matt Webb and Matt Jones, BERG explores the near future, creating products which open up connections between the digital world and the real, all with a sense of fun. An early work, Availabot, is a little model person connected to a computer via USB, who stands up straight when a particular friend comes online. Schooloscope reveals the complex and indigestible data of schools' league tables in the

Little Printer combines feeds from your smartphone to create personalised mini-newspapers.

form of little smiling buildings. Their latest project, Little Printer, seeks to combine the palpable usefulness of paper with the dynamic and content-rich nature of the web, printing out tiny personally-curated newspapers at the push of a button. With little orange legs and a smiling face, it points to a technological future that's playful, not slick or intimidating.

But what can architects stand to learn from this? With notable exceptions, the real potential of the digital world has so far passed us by; computers may have changed the way we work and the formal complexity of what we can build,

but we've largely failed to explore the consequences of technology on a social level. If architects are to enter this new terrain, BERG offer
a unique precedent of a design practice merging
the social and the technological.

As we look to the near future, it's fair to ask
'What comes next?' It's probably worth noting
that BERG stands for British Experimental
Rocket Group – I'm tipping it's jetpacks.

Conducted 30th November 2010 at the Architectural Association in London.

Rory Hyde: In your lecture you presented a definition
of design from your partner Jack Schulz, which simply states that 'design is about cultural invention'.
How does that cultural ambition shape the work you
produce?

Matt Webb: I don't have a design background, so one
of the things I'm curious about running this design
studio is 'What is design anyway?' To break it apart
for myself I started keeping a list of every time somebody used 'designer' as their job role, and I got up to
seven mutually incompatible descriptions. So I started
looking for other definitions of what design could
be. There's communication, product invention, understanding the world, design fiction – all these are
valid. But the one that best describes the thing that
we do, is we attempt to invent things and create
culture. It's not just enough to invent something and
see it once; you have to change the world around you,
get underneath it, interfere with it somehow, because
otherwise you're just problem-solving. And I won't say

that design has an exclusive hold over this – you can invent things and change culture with art, music, business practices, ethnography, market research; all of these are valid too – design just happens to be the way we do it.

RH: I like this idea of the designer who doesn't solve problems but who creates culture. Are you thinking about value when you are doing this, or are you more thinking about interestingness, or things that make you smile? Are you consciously out there trying to make products, or does that just happen by accident?

MW: I think the idea of products is really important. I have these things I look for in our work. One is hope; I think our things should be hopeful, and not just functional. Another is that it should be beautiful, inventive and mainstream. I think mainstream is important because otherwise you're just affecting a few people. A product is a good gate because you start to ask 'How is this going to be consumed by the market?' We don't have many ways of judging whether something is really good, and money is one of them. And that's kind of what products do.

I will say something about why to invent as well. Because you could see our work as experimental, or science fiction, or futuristic; but I would say – and others in the studio may not agree with me – that our design is essentially a political act. We design 'normative' products, normative being that you design for the world as it should be. Invention is always for the world as it should be, and not for the world you are in. By designing it, it's a bit like the way the earth attracts the moon, and the moon attracts the earth just a tiny bit. Design these products and you'll move the world just slightly in that direction.

The Near Future Inventor

RH: It also feels as though you're building on a long history; I mean, you talk about the practice being about the future, but a lot of slides you showed were of the history of design fiction – such as HAL from *2001*, the film *War Games*, and the incredible speculative images of a suburban future in space as imagined by NASA in the 1970s. What role does history play in the studio?

MW: I try not to make a distinction between things that are true and things that are fictional, because they all hang together in the same human brains. Anything, whether it's *2001*, or the history of Levittown, or what's on the market right now in the Argos catalogue is ripe for research. We're mining the same fields. Some things are conscious probes, so *2001* is a conscious probe into what it would be like to have a world where we're surrounded by artificial intelligence. Kubrick said that very specifically. *War Games* probably isn't the same kind of intellectual probe, but it works all the same because it hangs together as a story, and that means it's true, in a certain kind of way. I don't like to make a distinction between these things as research.

Image created from a long exposure of Penki, an app created for i-devices to paint words with light.

RH: Just to explore this Argos example further, in your presentation you said that 'the future is happening right now under our noses, and it's in the Argos catalogue', which you also referred to as the 'evolutionary soup' of product development. In particular you focused on cheap toys which employed what you termed as 'fractional AI'. What is fractional AI and how is it different to what we understand as regular artificial intelligence?

MW: The first thing I'll say is that the idea of Chinese manufacturers as an evolutionary soup is an idea of Bruce Sterling's from a short story. When you read the Argos catalogue, you get the feeling that things aren't being designed deliberately, but they're just throwing things at the wall and seeing what sticks, and that is a system for natural selection.

About 'fractional AI', I reference two things there. One is artificial intelligence as it is seen in movies of the mid-20th century: human-scale or larger intelligences as seen in books by Arthur C. Clarke or Isaac Asimov, for instance. But then there's this idea which emerged in the early 1900s of fractional horsepower. Horsepower used to be the thing that we measured factories by, but fractional horsepower says that instead of motors that are as big as buildings, we could have motors that are as big as fists. So we could take the fruits of these factories, make them really really tiny, and put them in our homes. Fractional horsepower enabled genuine improvements in quality of life, through appliances like washing machines, refrigerators and hairdryers. And we had half a million fractional horsepower motors in the US by the 1920s, it was an incredible explosion that made domestic life better.

My belief is that we're going to have the same explosion with artificial intelligence. And we won't see it as it was depicted in films as controlling nuclear weapons (*War Games*), or controlling space ships (*2001*). Fractional AI means that the tiny things around us will be smarter. And the very first place you see this in a very tiny way is in children's toys. It used to be that children played with Meccano or Lego, now they play The Sims. The Sims is a representation of a world in which everything is intelligent in really tiny ways, and we'll be seeing more of that I think in conventional products. What does an intelligent car look like? It may only be as intelligent as a puppy, so what does that mean?

RH: How much of the intelligence of an object or device do we bring to it ourselves? You also showed these photos of taps, power sockets or curtain rails which we read as faces, applying a personality at some deep emotional level to random inanimate stuff in the world. It seems like this step to making things smarter or more human or more magical is a very small one.

MW: We're already doing this; if you look at the fronts of cars, they look like faces. The arrangement of a bumper and two headlights can make a happy face, or a demanding face, or an exciting face, or an 'I want to go faster' face. We bring to these things our expectations of what faces mean, so yes, we bring a lot to it by our expectations. But it also points to the idea that there is a role for someone in the design of the personality, which is increasingly the behaviour of an object. So when we're designing a computer game, or a car, or an appliance, do we want it to make us feel like we can get involved more? Or that we have to be humble to it? Or that we're in a collaborative relationship? It used to be that we didn't think about these things, but we're going to have to think about how to design them soon. And I think that's happening right now.

RH: As someone trained in architecture – a literally very 'concrete' and often serious discipline – this idea that we need to design the emotions seems kind of exciting, and potentially frivolous. But I also feel like it shouldn't be. Is functionalism still far too dominant in how we approach design?

MW: We've experienced a shift in the last fiifty years, in that the bleeding edge of technology used to be industry, so the objects we got in our homes were the off-cuts of industry. Look at computers, or the mobile phone, or the internet; those came from industrial mainframes, or battlefield communications, or decentralised information systems. We've experienced a flip now; the technology we have starts on the desktop, in games consoles, or from texting your mates. That is the bleeding edge of technology, and it is leading the way. And it's quite unsurprising that the world we were trained to be in – the industrial one – was one that's a bit soulless, where you had to follow orders, be a cog in the machine. So maybe we're not quite trained right for the things we're being asked to design now, which start from the domestic sphere. Now that's incredibly exciting, because we get to look at other disciplines for where

Here and There, a speculative map projection for dense cities.

we should learn our craft, and maybe that's character animators, child psychologists, cartoonists, or architects of intimate domestic spaces instead of office buildings.

RH: Just to wrap up with one final question, we're here in the Architectural Association – have you got any advice for young designers about to graduate into the big wide world?

MW: One of the things that impressed me when I discovered the web was the number of architects who work on it. And I started asking them why they were so well adapted to work on the web, in this brand new medium. I got lots of different answers, but one of the things that struck me was that architects really understand how people – and specifically groups of people – respond to the structures and spaces around them and how they move through different spaces that have different expectations on them. We're going to be in a world where there's going to be brand new technology around us which responds to our expectations, and responds to our behaviour, which we will experience in groups. Architecture is fantastic training for that, so, know no boundaries.

THE
STRATEGIC
DESIGNER

Bryan
Boyer Helsinki
Design Lab

In 1969, Buckminster Fuller would publish his seminal work *Utopia or Oblivion*, mapping out two potential futures for humankind which had become simultaneously possible in the brief space of a number of years. On the one hand, innovations in the fields of information and energy opened up the possibility to solve our physical problems of existence by fulfilling the needs of all humanity. On the other, the development and proliferation of nuclear weapons made possible the precise opposite: our total annihilation. According to Fuller, what separated these two outcomes was the *design* of our systems of political decision-making.

Buckminster Fuller presenting his 'Dymaxion Airocean World' map of the earth as one continuous landmass at Helsinki Design Lab 1968.

One year prior, in 1968, Fuller joined a number of other visionary thinkers including Victor Papanek, Kaj Frank and Christopher Alexander for the inaugural Helsinki Design Lab (HDL), a conference directed to the changing role of the designer in meeting the demands of a new and complex world. Hosted by the nascent Finnish National Fund for Research & Development, now known as Sitra, the conference would promote design as an integrator between the previously distinct terrains of design and governance.

And it is this integrative approach to design and governance that Sitra continues to pursue today, an approach which has been stepped up with the revival of the Helsinki Design Lab more than forty years later. Run by the core team of Marco Steinberg, Justin Cook, Bryan Boyer and Dan Hill, the HDL exercise what they term 'Strategic Design', an approach to problem-solving which starts from an understanding of the complex and interrelated systems which shape our contemporary world. The team have an explicit remit to address the systemic challenges facing Finland, focusing in particular on the issues of education, sustainability and ageing.

But why Finland? Having been named nothing short of the 'best country in the world' by *Newsweek* (based on the criteria of health, economic dynamism, education and political environment), and with the capital Helsinki also ranked first in *Monocle*'s liveability index, what is there to worry about? Instead of using this apparent success as an excuse for complacency, Finland is pursuing a long-term anticipatory approach to the challenges of the future.

A key project of Sitra and HDL is Low2No, a €60 million mixed-use urban development near to Helsinki's centre which, through a combination of low embodied energy and on- and off-site energy production, will over time be carbon neutral. Importantly, Low2No is to be more than a mere 'demonstration' project – a term that implies the limited success of a heavily subsidised one-off – but will instead clear the path of overly burdensome bureaucratic or legal hindrances to encourage subsequent developments in its wake.

The threat of oblivion today is no longer that of mutually assured nuclear destruction, but the gradual liquidation of our planet's atmosphere. And yet just as Fuller posited, the systems of political decision-making continue to hold us back. By embedding designers within this process, and rethinking the architecture of decision-making, the Helsinki Design Lab are doing their small part to develop the tools that may push us collectively toward utopia.

Conducted 29th August 2011 at the offices of Sitra in Helsinki.

Rory Hyde: Let's start off with a real doozy: what is Strategic Design?

Bryan Boyer: If traditional design is about giving shape to objects or buildings, then Strategic Design is about giving shape to decisions. In the middle of the design spectrum there's the *making* of something – a chair, a book, a building – and there's a lot of decisions that come before the thing gets made, and there are a lot of decisions that the thing inflects after it enters the world. So being very aware of those sets of decisions within the design process is the role of the Strategic Designer.

RH: In your writing regarding the HDL you often refer to looking beyond the building or operating within a larger context – more abstract notions of strategy – but this definition sounds like Strategic Design still fundamentally revolves around *things.*

BB: This is a really prescient question in a way, and it's something that we're trying to sort through continually. The project, or the 'thing', is always an important part of how we frame our work; it's a kind of 'alibi' for the strategic or the systemic work that you want to do. So in the case of Low2No for example, ultimately it's about changing the practice of city-making, which means it touches building codes, finance models, lifestyles, economic development, construction methods, a whole number of things, few of which are tangible.

To put it in really blunt terms, the old theory of change would be 'Let's get a bunch of people to think about how to change the practice of city-making and determine what amendments we need and let's push them through as new regulations', all in the abstract. Whereas in our model, we use this very specific and tangible project, Low2No, to pursue our more abstract ambitions and changes we want to make.

So there's a kind of tether between the tangible thing and the abstract implications, and for us that's the interesting territory.

RH: Strategic Design seems to sit at the intersection of the spatial and the bureaucratic and explore how that combination of knowledge can allow us to make more informed decisions. What type of issues can this kind of thinking help us to address, and how is it relevant to Finland?

BB: To give you an example, in Finland, if you're an elderly person you are eligible to have food delivered to your home if you're unable to leave the house. As is the case in many countries. Now this is a pretty simple problem in a city like Helsinki, where the limits are well defined and the fabric is quite homogenous and dense. But if you go to a place like Jyväskylä the core is very dense but the periphery is very sparse; it's a radically different spatial condition, which then affects the ability for the city to honour that requirement to deliver food. So you can't consider how to feed the elderly of Jyväskylä unless you understand it as a decision that plays out over space and material, which is very complicated in the abstract space of Excel.

HDL's thinking operates on a national scale. Diagram of population change in Finland 2000–2007 in 100 km² grid.

The Strategic Design response would be to analyse the problem in its larger context. If it's too expensive to deal with this person on the periphery, maybe it's not about giving them the same service, but to offer them a place to move, or to work with their neighbour or family member to make sure they're taken care of. And so more and more of what we're seeing is the need to be that bridge between the tangible thing that you're trying to do, and how you do it; to challenge the way things are done and to open up new opportunities by really engaging material and spatial realities.

RH: It's interesting that the HDL is made up of architects. What kind of specific skills or ways of thinking do you think architects bring to these kinds of problems as distinct from other designers, and even from other disciplines such as policy or governance?

BB: OK, so this is also a key one. I think the fundamental thing that makes architecture an interesting training for this kind of work is that as an architect you are obliged to always balance the very hard, calculable, finite things like gravity and cost, with the soft incalculable cultural aspects, like aesthetics and the opinions of a community. This is something that you have in any field of design that has to deal with manufacturing, but the thing that I think differentiates architecture is the ability to do this at *scale*. And that as soon as you operate on such a scale, both physically and in terms of investment, you almost immediately have to engage economy and politics. No building is realised without some negotiation of those, whether it's at a family level – any domestic architect can tell you about the family politics that go into designing a house – or at the scale of a city or a nation. And therefore I think architecture is quite a useful starting point for these strategic

The Strategic Designer

pursuits, because again you cannot operate strategically in the absence of economy or politics.

RH: To that I'd also add timescales. Practically any piece of architecture takes years from start to finish, which forces you to become a shepherd of ideas, to negotiate the various hoops of bureaucracy and money and politics even.

BB: Exactly, and I think it's good to call it out as something explicit, I was sort of nesting it within economy and politics, but I think you're right. You also asked about how it differentiates from other fields of design as well as non-design fields, and I think that's a key one too, where I would criticise some

The HDL Studio program brought together experts from diverse fields for week-long intensives.

of the language around Design Thinking as being *greedy* in terms of what they claim as the native territory of the designer. So for instance, 'creativity' is absolutely *not* something that only designers can claim; it doesn't matter what you're practising, of course you can be creative.

And I actually think that – and I don't bring it up just to trash design thinking – if we want to be effective in these larger conversations about what Strategic Design practice looks like, or why we even need Strategic Design, or what roles designers can play in these larger conversations, we really have to be able to articulate what we can do that other people are not as well equipped to do. And that shouldn't be something which is a huge grab-bag of different qualities and abilities, it should be something very

Bryan Boyer

specific. Of course you can also be specific at being fuzzy; your ability might be being able to engage other kinds of disciplines, which is also a key one for architecture.

RH: For me it's a really important point, because on the one hand specificity is often cited as a reason for architects' increasing irrelevance or redundancy; we've become such effective 'stylists' that we're no longer invited to participate in these other more strategic aspects of a project.

BB: For me it's more about where we *haven't* been proactive; that's what has really shaped the contemporary role of the architect rather than where we *have* been proactive. So it's not that we've advanced the discipline of form-making so far and are so articulate about it and we're just so brilliant, it's actually that we're *not* able to have a conversation about why we made these forms and what these forms do. By not being able to articulate even in some basic way how our practice operates, we've cut ourselves out of other conversations.

RH: What do we need to do to achieve this broader acceptance of what we do? To quote from your *Perspecta* piece, you state that 'universities are not making explicit the value of architecture beyond its cultural contribution', and go on to mention all the aspects we avoid such as post-occupancy evaluation and scientific research.[25] Should we be employing more hard facts or metrics to justify what we do? Have we exhausted the credibility of aesthetic persuasion?

BB: In this age of globalised architecture, you have so many new layers in the process that the relationship is no longer between the architect as visionary and the client with faith, so we've had to develop new tools of being persuasive. That's where I see the contemporary use of the diagram fitting in, it's really used as a tool of *battle*, and I put it in those terms very specifically, because large-scale projects are a form of modulated battle. A number of practices work this way, particularly OMA and their hyper-rational offshoots; the diagram becomes a tool for the client presentation to win arguments as quickly and easily as possible. The bulk of what has been written about diagrammatic architecture is still on the side of the diagram as a tool internal to the design process, but we can also observe its use as a tool of communication – and ultimately a way to persuade clients that a design decision was inevitable. Elsewhere some practices are digging deeper into the *pro forma* of the work they're asked to take on, so here we find the budget and profit projections of the project being anointed as construction documents. And there's a growing use of narrative again in the presentation of architecture. For me this collectively points to a moment of exploration in how architecture is conducted as a practice and what it aspires to deliver. In that sense my hope is that we see each method as tools rather than process dogma, and as a community we become more strategic about how, when and why we apply these specific tools.

RH: It's probably useful at this point to talk more about some specific projects of HDL. I'm interested in discussing how the Low2No competition was run so as to encourage a broader set of competencies beyond those of architectural effects, such as the capacities of the team, sustainability credentials, etc.

Bryan Boyer

BB: Fundamentally Low2No was launched as a request for qualifications (RFQ), that list was scored as it always is, and from there we selected five teams to advance to a second stage. For this second stage the teams had to deliver an explanation of their capacities and experience, a strategy manual, and their draft design proposal in the form of boards. As with any procurement, the question was 'How do we do this in a way that it doesn't just come down to cost?' So the criteria was really about the mix, and proving that your team could deliver the best result.

Low2No design development illustration.

Despite all this emphasis on strategy, the architectural proposals were also very important, and I think it goes back to the start of the conversation about the 'alibi'. Because as wonderful as a strategy manual is, the result of Low2No is a big physical chunk of the city, so we need that visual tool to communicate this broader set of concerns. As a pair the design boards and the strategy manual are a really effective combo. If you try to imagine it without the building, it's just harder to have that conversation. The fact that at some point there's going to be tonnes and tonnes of concrete and steel and jobs – all of that very real and tangible stuff going on – brings an added urgency.

What we're specifically looking at through the Strategic Design program is 'How can the project be the alibi for urgency?' So for example, we're having discussions now about the use of timber in large-scale construction, which has all sorts of benefits in terms of carbon capture and the core industries of Finland,

The Strategic Designer

but is currently impossible under the building code as it stands.* Being able to say 'There's this thing happening, it's going to be here in 2015, and if you don't get your act together you're going to miss out' is a great way to bring meaningful urgency to regulatory or policy conversations which are required to push through changes at a systemic level. The strategic implications come in pursuing these conversations at that level, rather than looking for a special allowance. This is what separates Strategic Design from the crafty pursuit of exemptions. So underneath all this rhetoric of the 'tether between the physical and the abstract', ultimately it just comes back to a very human way of working. In the face of potentially great change, we just need something to point at.

* HDL have subsequently been successful in revising the building code to allow the large-scale construction of timber buildings.

RH: This example of the timber industry and changing the building code seems to be a useful one, and it highlights the unique position that Sitra holds within government. I'm interested in how you use this position as a way to make changes to policy in order to clear the way for others so that Low2No is not just a demonstration project.

BB: Essentially, Sitra reports to parliament, but we have an independent endowment. Which, as you point out, is a very unique position to have. It means that we have the remit and requirement to think about things on a national scale, and it means that we have the independence and ability to pursue things that aren't yet urgent, but will be. So in one sense, our agenda is to drive urgency toward topics which we predict will have a strategic importance for Finland. So while we focus on projects such as Low2No, we're

Bryan Boyer

not a property developer; these projects have to contain a plausible opportunity to produce systemic change for Finland.

Yes that's very vague, but basically it means the ambition has to be higher. When we set out to do this project, a large-scale timber building was illegal, but we gave ourselves the freedom to imagine that this wasn't the case, especially as if that law was changed, it could change the system, and open up a whole range of opportunities in its wake. So we're interested in these things that have the potential to reverberate beyond our site. Our interest is not just in the success of this project, but in the health of this sector of Finnish industry.

The Strategic Designer

THE MANAGEM ENT THINKERS

Todd Reisz

on consultants

The brochure on the services offered by the global consulting mega-firm Pricewaterhouse-Coopers to their clients in the Middle East includes 'master site planning, functional planning, capacity analysis, space programming, materials analysis and schematic designs'.[26] Now, isn't this what architects used to do?

The position of the architect at the top of the food chain in determining the shape of the built environment has been under relentless assault for centuries. To find examples of an integrated architect with absolute authority, one has to go back to Vitruvius' description of the 'architektura' as designer-engineer from 15 BC, the 'master builders' of the Renaissance, or the cathedral builders of the Middle Ages. The rise in the complexity of the city – from simple shelters to 'machines for living' – has seen a parallel rise in specialisation, with the core services offered by the architect progressively encroached upon by dozens of new professions.

The latest stage in this evolution of the complexity of cities is the shift from simply being designed to deliver quality of life, to becoming speculative instruments of economic investment. In turn, governments and rulers are now turning to financial and management consultants for

Todd Reisz

advice instead of urbanists or architects. This is particularly true in the Gulf region of the Middle East, where the likes of Pricewater-houseCoopers and McKinsey & Co. are increasingly engaged in the process of city-making.

The most audacious example of this new role of the management consultant is McKinsey's $60 billion plan for six Economic Cities in Saudi Arabia. The largest of these, King Abdullah Economic City (KAEC), will stretch over 173 km^2, become home to two million people, create one million jobs, and cost a staggering $27 billion.[27]

When viewed from a business perspective, it makes sense to employ those with experience in global finance and investment for a project such as this. It's hardly celebrated by the planning or architectural professions, as these new rivals encroach on profits and influence. However, defending the traditional territory of the architect or urbanist is certainly a fruitless task; and besides, if our competitors are more enterprising and better equipped to deliver these kinds of projects, surely we only have ourselves to blame.

But as this interview with architect and expert on the urban history of the Gulf, Todd Reisz, explores, if we are to put professional self-interest aside, and objectively examine the impact these consultants leave on the ground, a more disconcerting picture appears. As cities are increasingly treated as investment vehicles, they run the risk of overlooking the needs of the people who will eventually live in these urban spreadsheets. Thus, this development should be treated by the traditional disciplines of urban design and archi-

Aerial view of Dubai in the mid 1960s as the first paved roads and infrastructure is constructed.

tecture as both a warning for what is to come, and an opportunity to form constructive coalitions to promote the qualities of public space and architecture that lie at our core.

Conducted 9th November at Todd's studio in Amsterdam.

Rory Hyde: Consulting in the Gulf region of the Middle East has a complex modern history. In a way, the cities we know today, Dubai, Abu Dhabi, Doha and Manama were built by consultants, by a culture of advice. Who first came here and for what reason?

> Todd Reisz: Well, much of this region was part of the British Empire under a so-called 'special treaty relation'. But it wasn't until after World War II that the British really came ashore. Up to that point there had

been British representation on shore, but it was only to meddle in the sheikhdoms' foreign affairs. At the end of World War II you have increased commercial interests in oil, so there is a greater concern on the side of the British government to protect their sovereignty in the region. And that means they have to ensure there is a semblance of domestic organisation. If you look at Dubai, Abu Dhabi, Bahrain, Qatar, they are surrounded by states forming, you have Iraq, Iran and Saudi Arabia; they are quickly becoming solidified in terms of statehood, with boundaries, with bureaucrats, with institutions of government. So the idea is that actually creating cities – meaning the institutions of cities, as opposed to the streetscapes – is essential. And so the question is how to do that. For the British that starts in places where oil was first found, Kuwait and Bahrain, but it was

Sheikh Rashid [bin Saeed Al Maktoum] in Dubai who was eventually the most open to change.

RH: Let's talk about Sheikh Rashid because he sounds like a pretty interesting character – the transitional figure between the old Dubai and the Dubai we know today.

TR: Yes, it's often proposed that he is the great visionary who foresaw the potential of modernisation as a way to make life better in Dubai. And I think that's essentially true, but in this case modernisation, and this includes the establishment of city governance, was a political

British consultant architect John Harris presents the original low-rise version of the World Trade Centre to Sheikh Rashid, 1973.

The Management Thinkers

move on the part of the British as well. The British negotiated it as a way to balance the interests of Dubai's royal family and its merchant families.

RH: So when did the infrastructural modernisation take place? And what course did it take?

TR: 1955, I would say, that's when the person who I'm calling the 'first consultant' comes to Dubai. Although he's Iraqi, he's invited by the British government. He essentially comes to look around the city, make some observations, and give a report. He's not that important in the end; he says he'll be back, and like many consultants he never comes back. But because of him there was a proper attendance to the idea that a butcher's shop had to be 'flywired', as they say, so public health regulation comes in, a garbage collection service begins, etc. And around the same time the British engineering firm Halcrow are working on the proposal to save Dubai's harbour. And that's essentially the triggering story of modernisation for Dubai: reinforcing the harbour and turning it into a more profitable port.

RH: It's interesting to consider the scale of investment to create this global hub for trade. It already shows a view to the outside world and a connection to global flows as an economic lifeline, which remains the model today.

TR: The thing is those global flows were already in Dubai at this stage. Even before the 20th century, Dubai understood its existence as based on the notion of global connections, and that is an essential story. Dubai was a global city before anyone was talking about global cities. Its existence depended upon the wealth of others. So in that regard, it's not such a

Todd Reisz

strange moment. But it is the first time that measurements are starting to be made in Dubai. These British engineers arrive and begin from scratch, literally designating the points from which the city is measured.

RH: You tell a great story in your *Log* piece about John Harris who is trained as an architect, but really finds himself doing planning.[28] He commissions the first aerial survey of Dubai and presents his proposal to Sheikh Rashid directly on top of it.

TR: Yes, Rashid had never seen an aerial photograph of his city. The two – the present and the future – are presented to him for the first time together. It's a beautiful moment. When I first saw the Harris plan, I thought it was unique, a rejection of a lot of traditional British town planning. But in another regard it is attached to the Garden City movement, also to Patrick Geddes; it asserts how the modern needs to move into the pre-modern, and find ways of establishing relationships.

RH: So we have Harris who's an architect planning Dubai, and to look at the Gulf more generally, we have Bechtel, these American engineers who come from an oil and civil engineering background designing these industrial cities in Saudi Arabia in the 1970s. Where were the planners in all this?

TR: There clearly were British planners in Saudi Arabia before Bechtel arrived. You also had Doxiadis in Riyadh, and you had British planners especially in Jeddah. But that's basically right, there's even a piece in the *RIBA Journal* by a planner from what would eventually become RMJM, who was scared that the role of the planner would disappear because of the dominating presence of American engineering companies. The whole issue is speed, and the kind of optimism that's imbued in unadulterated infrastructure. At this stage of the game, the British planner's fear was well founded; production of infrastructure became everything. The planners ended up reporting to the engineers.

RH: Why do you think these engineers are preferred over the planners? Because they present a non-designed approach which is purely functional; the city treated as a machine, rather than as a place to live perhaps?

TR: The beginnings of their success is not actually in the city, but in ports, in pipes, and oil rigs. Those successes enable them to be seen as the people who get things done. Halcrow modernises the port of Jeddah, and suddenly Jeddah has the capacity to increase the number of visitors for the Hajj. Bechtel was doing the same on Saudi Arabia's other shore and developing the Trans-Arabian Pipeline, Saudi Arabia's ultimate lifeline to wealth. Both of these examples are about machinery. It's not until later that you see that the engineers are specifically coming to the cities and working with planners.

Jubail Industrial City, Saudi Arabia.

RH: You have this great description of Bechtel's proposal for Jubail, which sounds almost like Sim City: very discreet zoning, industrial, commercial, residential, all very evenly spread out. There seems to be a simplicity in their approach – a sort of *tabula rasa* – which I wonder if you think is more appropriate than these models of elaborate planning imported from Europe?

TR: I think before asking whether they're appropriate, it's important to note that these plans are all derived from British town planning anyway. So the engineers are not inventing this stuff, they're simply divorcing it from a kind of theory and attachment to history. The engineer strips planning of this baggage and lets it appear as common sense. It's an obsession with logistics, with calculations, and looking as the city as an economic machine. By this time, in the 1970s, urban planners had rightfully jettisoned this high-modernist approach based on unsuccessful experiences. Engineers, however, had found a new life for high modernism in the Gulf.

RH: Perhaps we should move on to today. When we speak of consultants working in the Gulf, we now implicitly mean management consultants. The building blocks are there, and now it's about fine-tuning these machines to make more money. Or even to build whole new cities to make money, such as these 'Economic Cities' in Saudi Arabia. So, firstly, what is an Economic City?

TR: 'Economic City' is a term being used by Saudi Arabia's national planners, likely originating from work produced by McKinsey & Co. Economic Cities are Saudi Arabia's next approach to city-building following its Industrial Cities of the 1970s. Industrial Cities were a way of building up a national economy – by making sure that as much money was being extracted from the country's oil drilling as possible. Economic Cities are also about producing economic growth, but today it's through the service industry and the knowledge economy. And there is a belief that global corporations, invested in Saudi resources and people, will fund it.

RH: So they're centred around universities, as well as special-use business districts which have certain tax conditions, or investment or living conditions.

TR: Exactly, at least that's the idea. Energy industries, however, still play a heavy role. In Saudi Arabia, there are examples where islands of exclusivity have been made in order to test social change; now that is taking the shape of fully functioning cities, or new urban districts. There is King Abdullah Economic City (KAEC), which is a half-hour from Jeddah, and supposed to be a sort of 'mirror experience' of Jeddah. Jeddah is an old city. It's known for its traffic, and congestion, and things not getting done. You've read about the horrific floods, so there's this sort of age-old notion of a broken city. KAEC is where things work, where kids can leave their apartments by themselves to go across the street to the playground. You have another one which is pretty much attached to the holy city of Medina where non-Muslims can get as close as possible to people living and working in Medina. It is supposed to generate a knowledge-based economy and a place where Saudis can be trained for service-based employment.

RH: And what role are consultants playing in determining these cities?

TR: As far as I know, McKinsey designated six Economic Cities in Saudi Arabia as a way of approaching national economic health and creating new jobs. McKinsey didn't make drawings, but they did work with the government on the idea of identifying new cities. And there is evidence they worked on developing the programming for at least some of the Economic Cities.

Todd Reisz

RH: So in a way they are working on the business plan for the *possibility* of a city. And you say 'as far as I know', which refers to the anonymity with which these advisors operate.

> TR: Right, compared to architects who try to promote their work by marketing what they've done, management consultants often take the other track of silence, as a way to protect success, let's say. There have always been times when architects have been anonymous or more anonymous, and we've seen positive effects from that. But for management consultants it's far more common to have silence clauses in contracts, where they are working in the service of someone else. I've only ever heard a representative from one Economic City explicitly say this was the idea of McKinsey.[29]

RH: What does that silence or anonymity enable them to do? Are they able to wash their hands of responsibility for the outcome? Or to be able to work for multiple clients?

> TR: It's an issue of authorship, right. You could say they are avoiding authorship and therefore avoiding responsibility, or on the other hand you could say they are not concerned with authorship. We know this with architects that there is an obsession with authorship, to the point that it breaks down the potential of an architectural or urban plan because of that obsession. If you look at this bizarre obsession that architects can possess for Brasília or Chandigarh for instance. These are heavily authored plans. There's an obsession with the ability to have been an author. Even still, should a consultant be allowed to remain anonymous? That's not necessarily right either…

The Management Thinkers

RH: And surely it relates to the fees they can set as well. As an architect or planner you are charging for your results, for a percentage of construction cost or a percentage of a proposal. Whereas, if you are just selling advice in the shadows, what you can charge is potentially unlimited.

TR: Well, I've definitely seen architects use contracts similar to management consultants, looking at phases, looking at reports issued – we've adopted their strategies to an extent. I think in this whole new idea of 'research', that architects do research and produce reports, it's not very far from what a management consultant will provide for a client. But who gets paid more? We can probably guess the answer.

RH: That taps into the resentment that architects and planners have toward management consultants moving into their territory by shaping cities. Should we be worried, or should we just adopt more of their strategies, learn to play their game? Or are we no longer suited for that role? Has planning become something altogether different, more about economics than about space?

TR: What I always find interesting between management consultants and architects is that they both profess to be generalists. They will comment on things broadly. The architect can talk to you about the details of a chair right up to expounding on Mumbai, the scale is limitless. The management consultant, if you look at what they do, they can talk to you about cities today as well as middle-class women's shopping experiences in the suburbs. One of them is doing it better than the other, right? What the management consultant has been able to do is to show this spectrum of generalisation is something that works in understanding the complexity of a city, as opposed to how the architect has approached being a generalist. It's a question of scale for the architect, but for the management consultant it's a question of breadth of economic conditions for the city. Which one do you find more vital?

RH: And in that sense it's understandable that the clients or the rulers are turning to these kinds of disciplines for advice – I would! The real questions are what is the impact once it hits the ground, what are the characteristics of these cities, and are they lacking because of who has been determining them in the first place, people who aren't trained in spatial planning? Of course they commission the architects and planners to work with them, but can we draw a line between the spatial qualities of these new cities and the ways in which they are initially proposed?

TR: An essential question to ask is 'Who is determining whether a particular economic city is important or necessary?' There was a point in urban planning's development in the 1970s when it was letting go of the physical characteristics of a city, what we call today 'urban design', and looked more at the economic conditions, the global networking that goes into how a city is planned. The planners essentially became more theoretical than visual. But what's happened since then is that the planner has lost that role of working with, let's say, the five-year development plans for a country and that's been taken over by others. So just as they caught on, they lost their audience. And it's not just the management consultants who've taken the stage, it's also the banks.

Look at demographic reports of regions where there are incredible amounts of urban growth.

Sometimes demographics are provided to you by banks – how disturbing is that? Banks have everything to gain from predictions of growth, they gain from both sides, they get commissioned to write that report, and then when everyone comes to apply for a mortgage. The consultant isn't doing it in the same way.

RH: Perhaps we can move on to the relationship between the consultants and the clients. I'm interested in this stereotypical attitude held by foreign consultants that the rulers have more money than sense, that they spend indiscriminately. To use Dubai as an example, it's a view somewhat reinforced by the comments of Sheikh Mohammed on *60 Minutes* when he says that he ignores the advice of his consultants when they contradict his own aims, and just says 'do it anyway'.[30] But this dynamic seems too simplistic considering what's been achieved. Who is really holding the power here?

TR: In a way this has become the standard mythology of the Gulf and specifically of Dubai. Like Sheikh Rashid in the 1960s being told his port should have five berths, and he decides it should be nine and in the end he builds eleven, and he was right. The consultant represents conventional wisdom. The management report always comes with a clause along the lines of 'decisions are being based on a historical pattern', and therefore the moment of incredibility won't be factored in. Yet there were moments of incredibility in Dubai that did happen, and whether Sheikh Rashid knew that they were coming or not, that's a question. Same with Sheikh Mohammed. I can't comment on what Sheikh Mohammed says, but I don't think he's necessarily talking about consultants so much as about the confines of conventional wisdom.

RH: This idea that Dubai is somehow the exception to all rules. This exceptionalism seems to have the other effect of also allowing you to *dismiss* Dubai. From the beginning it's never been perceived as a 'real' city; it's always been either too small, built too fast, or now perceived as being too different and so somehow not real. Why are these cities still perceived as being provisional, and is that part of the strategy?

> TR: Dubai's apparent incompletion has often been to its advantage. There is value in not yet being established, because it allows people to come in and fill in the blanks, to find their role in the bonanza. As to being provisional, what often startles me is that critics assume other cities are forever. In fact, all cities are provisional.

RH: You have a great quote from an architect from Lebanon who is working in Dubai, who says 'this place is crazy but it's also really boring'.

> TR: Which is true. Expressed ambitions might at times seem crazy, but in the end I think Dubai's leaders are very much striving for completion and establishment. That's really what infrastructure allowed. I wrote about establishing the roots by means of concrete piles in the ground, that's more than a metaphor; it becomes real. Dubai does not want to drift away, and that wish is great but pretty mundane.

RH: That also refers to the more recent disparagement of this provisionalism from the Western media. With the crisis all the headlines would read 'cities reclaimed by the desert' or 'the rats come in'.[31] I guess we are seeing a shift now from the intentionally provisional as a way to attract migrants, as a way to attract workers, or business, to a need to convince the world that this is a real place now.

> TR: Yes, I still think you have moments of excitement and creation in the Gulf, Doha for instance, which has been quiet for decades, and suddenly with the World Cup coming in ten years, its agenda becomes more clear. Every day there is news about billions of dollars being put into such and such an infrastructure project. There is always a need for a story like that in real-estate development media, and the Gulf seems always able to provide that headline. Dubai, on the other hand, now has too much – too much office space, too much housing, things are vacant, there is emptiness. And now Dubai can turn around to a world that's been criticising it for going too fast, and say 'Oh, but a city takes time'. It's a nice twist, and they're right. Interestingly enough, it has been Dubai's ability to attract foreigners to stay for longer terms that will be the lesson for Doha.

RH: Maybe we should conclude with the current status. Obviously the financial crisis seemed to shake up this once very symbiotic relationship between foreign consultants and the work that needed doing. The media breathlessly reported on expats who went bankrupt and ended up in jail, or just fled leaving their Porsches at the airport. Is the love affair over? And is that why we are seeing these new knowledge cities, to train local talent to take over this role?

A consultant desperately advertises his 'experience in mega projects' at Dubai's Cityscape real-estate fair, 2009.

> TR: I think there are definitely examples where there is a drive to build a local

knowledge base. This idea has been around since even the 1950s, whether in agriculture, trade, banking or oil. There are now more examples, like Education City in Doha, also universities in Abu Dhabi and Dubai. But at the same time what is shocking about the financial crisis is that there is a whole new level of consultants coming in: the financial consultants who are negotiating between the debtors and the creditors, the PR people wanting to help Dubai fix its image. There are people who call themselves 'reputation consultants' who try to convince people to help them re-establish themselves and their legitimacy. There's always room for new consultants.

RH: It's a nice trajectory to trace through these past fifty odd years, to go from the very physical civil engineering of ports and highways and water pipes, to the most intangible advice on reputation and PR.

TR: Yes, it's true, but it's not like it was a marvellous or optimistic time back then either. If you look back at the engineering, there is a lot still missing in terms of what makes a real city, and there were a lot of mistakes made as well. 'Cities as machines' – you can't really say that about the Gulf anymore...

THE COMMUNITY ENABLER

Marcus Westbury

Renew Newcastle

The late British architect Cedric Price, irritated by the bickering of a husband and wife who had approached him to design their new house, famously scolded them by saying 'You don't need a new house, you need a divorce!' Architects like this line, firstly because it's funny, secondly because it capture's Price's ambivalence toward his clients in turning down a commission, but most of all because it acknowledges that a new building isn't always the answer, and places our work within the fragile contingencies of human relationships.

But it's strange that we like it, because it also exposes the limit of the architect's power, the limits of our capacity to create social change through spatial means. It suggests that no matter how socially conducive the design of a house is, it's not powerful enough to save a marriage. But can design can be powerful enough to save a *street*?

It was this conviction that motivated the city planners of Newcastle, Australia to renovate the public spaces of the Hunter Street Mall, a shopping strip in decline, plagued by vacant tenancies and a frequent target of arson. Millions of dollars were spent on repaving the plaza, planting new street trees and installing new benches,

Marcus Westbury

Before: Renew Newcastle negotiates access to a commercial tenancy on Hunter Street Mall that had been vacant for seven years.

After: Vox Cyclops, a creative project as part of Renew Newcastle, combining record store, studio and gallery space.

all with little impact in reviving the activity or commercial potential of this decaying strip.

Then, in 2009, along came Renew Newcastle, a not-for-profit organisation established to fill these vacant spaces with local artists, designers and craftspeople, and ultimately to 'renew' the creative potential of the city. Founder Marcus Westbury identified the problem facing the Hunter Street Mall not as spatial – if anything, space was in abundance – but as economic, legal and policy-related. Building owners were reluctant to let their vacant spaces be used in case they were approached by a full-paying tenant, while many prospective tenants were deterred from renting the spaces by the high upfront capital requirements and insurance costs.

By developing a unique tenancy agreement based on rolling short-term periods, and by acting as an intermediary organisation providing security for other legal requirements, Renew Newcastle has been able to find spaces for dozens of cultural projects, and regenerated the life of the street. The idea has since taken off in a number of other cities across the country, with Westbury now establishing Renew Australia to coordinate these various projects.

Notably, Westbury is not an architect (he has a background as a director of arts festivals and as a cultural commentator), but he is included here to illustrate the potential of non-architectural strategies in achieving very architectural outcomes. The community enabler deploys the ample resource of *people* as a catalyst for change, where spatial improvements may be ineffective. If architects were to expand their toolkits to include strategies like those of Renew, the potential to create social change would be greatly magnified. Who knows, we might even be able to save a marriage.

Conducted 10th April 2011 at A Minor Place café in Melbourne.

Rory Hyde: I found a great quote where you describe yourself as 'part frustrated architect, part under-capitalised property developer, part town planner of fictional utopias, part the most petty of petty dictators'.[32] It's obviously fairly tongue in cheek, but raises

the question of how you see your role, and how your
background as an organiser of arts festivals informed
the thinking that went into Renew Newcastle?

Marcus Westbury: Renew Newcastle is about practical
experiments and constraints; it doesn't start with a
theoretical underpinning, it's about trial and error.
The background I brought to this project was simply
living in Newcastle as it was falling apart, while
simultaneously being surrounded by a very active
community who had very little money. I realised the
absence of a connection between empty space and
people who want to animate it was the basic problem.
This ticked over in the back of my mind for about ten
years, and eventually led to Renew.

I also became skeptical of the process of bringing
in experts from outside, who offered up these grand
visions in response to this dysfunctional place. I used
to go to these workshops with consultants who had
worked in Manchester or Dublin, and they would
show these beautiful plans of bars and café tables and
say this is what could happen here. And I'd take one
look at it and say 'That's actually illegal in this state,
you can't have small bars'. Between the people running the planning process and the people running
the consultancies offering up the visions, no one actually just looked at the rules and said what's possible.

My starting point is to ask 'Can we do this here?'
And out of that you can grow all these other things.
If you can lower the barrier of entry to 'what you
can do here' you can organically generate some of the
structured outcomes which would fail to manifest
despite all the resources thrown at them in the world.

RH: That links to your idea of software versus hardware as this applies to cities.[33] I'm going to quote you

The Community Enabler

again if that's allowed: 'many who seek to use the city are attempting to do little more than run a virus – a parasite of a program – called Maximising_my_commercial_return.exe'. Cities have become just about money, rather than opportunities. Can we put up a firewall and allow other programs to run which might be more culturally focused, for instance?

MW: Just to explain this hardware/software idea a little further. So at one end you've got the hardware, the hard physical infrastructure of the city – most people who are interested in cities think of them in this way, they build things, they want to physically redesign them – and at the other end of the spectrum you've got the software, the users who want to make things happen, and all these rules in between dictating what's allowed and what's possible. And some of those rules are fixed – such as policy – they are the hard rules in a city which create boundaries which are as firm as the boundaries of hard infrastructure. If the rules don't allow it, you can't do it, and unless you change the rules, it won't happen. So my starting point is to explore how these rules respond to people without capital.

These rules are largely designed to constrain capital; to constrain people with too much money from behaving inappropriately in a way that exploits those around them. One of the simplest things to do is create a rule which obliges people to spend money to achieve some social outcome – like retrofitting a building for disability access, or soundproofing – so in a lot of ways these rules address legitimate problems, but they also add an additional layer of cost and complexity which shuts out people who don't have capital. My question is, what are the opportunities for people who don't have capital? And what structures can you put in place to make those opportunities work? Can we create societies where we don't need money to play, or at least not a lot of money, in order to do something?

RH: So your response is not about giving people money, but about giving people the opportunity to play within this system and to arrive at the aim that they want, which may be to make art, or to open a small creative business.

MW: And sometimes just to experiment, I'm obsessed with the idea of experimentation. So rather than this idea of predetermining any sort of successful or unsuccessful process that's going to work, we've done sixty experiments in Newcastle. If you can just let sixty experiments run, you are inevitably going to find out what works best through trial and error. And that's a much more democratic way of doing it than just offering one solution.

RH: This is one of the things I really like about Renew; you've got a whole spectrum of projects, like the Mad Hatters, and people who are really crafty, who perhaps in a traditional arts funding model would be pushed outside. It doesn't seem like you bring a preconceived value judgement about what's 'good'.

MW: It's quite important that it's diverse, because you're trying to get a broad cross-section of the community to support it, and you want a wide cross-section of the community to be interested in the city again. So, it's not about me picking a dozen projects that I find cool and interesting, it's actually about creating a mechanism that facilitates a really wide range of things. We've got a food co-op, we've got a stack of visual art galleries, studios, publishers, graphic designers, the ladies making hats, and everything in between. That's quite integral to the success of the model. If it's going to be resilient, it can't just be dependent on a particular whim or sub-section of the community for support.

RH: Another strength is the speed of it, the ability for tenants and owners to get in and out of the program easily. But I'm interested in what your long-term prospects might be; what do you dream of at night that this might turn into? I feel like the title is a clue, it's very ambitious: *Renew* Newcastle. The city as the project.

MW: The city is the project in a lot of ways, but the individual projects are the project as well. One way I describe it is that it's a 'permanent structure for temporary things'. So Renew Newcastle is permanent, but the projects are temporary. That doesn't mean they have to be temporary, it just means we are not trying to design them, they have to do that for themselves. In my experience of arts and cultural projects and with small business people, most projects fail. Our goal is to plant lots of seeds and give each a chance to start and grow, not to make a list at the beginning and ensure that each will be there in five years. Having said that, there are a dozen projects which have been there since day one, or have either moved on and are now viably paying commercial rent.

To return to the point about the city, just by bringing in all these projects you are giving a new character to a place; you are changing what it is by doing it, not by arguing about it. These projects now define the character of an area, they define a space, they set

Marcus Westbury

examples of what can and can't happen, which is very different from an argument about whether you should bulldoze that site and build a new development on it. You are creating reality by doing it. That brings life back, that brings commerce back.

RH: The project is very specific, in that it responds to some very particular issues which Newcastle faces, but in a way those issues are part of a larger trend: the decline of industry and the rise of knowledge work. I know you've been talking about this around Australia, and also around the world, in the US for instance. Do you see the Renew 'model' being exported? Can it be successful in other cities?

MW: Yes, I think you are already seeing evidence of it being successful in other cities. It depends on how you measure success too. In Newcastle's case, it has generated additional layers of effect, in terms of publicity and promotion for the city. On a basic level, the very simple mechanism of giving the creative community opportunities by brokering access to empty space as a way to activate a precinct, works pretty much anywhere you want to do it. The extent to which it works, whether you achieve the scale of result you would have achieved in Newcastle, I'm not entirely sure about.

RH: And as you mentioned earlier, it has grown out of your personal experience of this place. Which perhaps brings us back to the idea of 'roles', and what kind of disciplines or professions might be best suited to set up a project such as this. While I'm wary of generalisations, I can't see an architect thinking in this way in response to a brief to revive an ageing commercial strip for instance. And in any case, they're not.

MW: I'm more interested in processes than outcomes, in how things happen rather than what the end result is. And I think most disciplines in this area are about end results. If you can think about – I keep using these words all the time – processes, mechanisms, software structures that facilitate the agency of lots of different people, that is what I'm interested in.

RH: Compared to the bricks and mortar of architecture's traditional self-conception, these are pretty intangible concerns. One of the key barriers for architects expanding their scope to include this territory is getting paid. Currently we're most often paid as a percentage of building cost, and that very fact alone means that any project that doesn't require new building is off our radar; it's not something we're interested in pursuing. Even though the aim might be to just 'renew' a place, unless you can develop a project brief that requires new work, then you don't get paid.

MW: And I should point out, it's very hard to get paid! [laughs] This is probably one of the very key starting points for Renew Newcastle, that I'm the first person who has done anything about this city in years who wasn't getting paid, and was happy to not get paid. And therefore I didn't have to deliver what someone would pay me to do, I just got a chance to generate what I thought would work. That is an incredible luxury to have, albeit a very expensive luxury, I funded it on my credit card! We had pro-bono lawyers, and a lot of good people donated their time and energy, but it was a long time before we saw a cent from anyone.

But now I am trying to get paid as I start to work for other places. That does change the balance a bit. It would be interesting to sit down to have this conversation again in five years time as I am increasingly working as a paid consultant, and see how that influences the practicalities of what I can and can't do. I don't think it would influence what I think is a good and bad idea, but it may do down the track. I can already see circumstances where it forces you into scenarios that are less than ideal, because, you know, that's what the brief demands of you. I've been very fortunate not to have had that constraint so far.

RH: In a sense, I can imagine architects, planners and city officials being *threatened* by what you've achieved with such minimal resources; it challenges their monopoly on creating social change at an urban scale. What has been the response from these groups?

MW: Pretty positive on the whole. It's been weird. I'm provocative but not confrontational. I want to put

ideas out there, but I don't want to start a fight with people. I tend to provoke in a 'I'm not having a go at your power' kind of way. I don't think you need to tear something down to build something up, I don't see the obvious point in doing that.

Crowds of people in Hunter Street Mall during the Red Lantern Night Market, 2009.

RH: Yes, there will always be different methods to shape the city which can coexist.

MW: This is a toolkit for people, it's a set of tools, strategies, mechanisms and ideas which I think they – architects, urban planners, people responsible for the future of the evolution of spaces, places, communities – should embrace and work with more. I think that it's an area not particularly well understood, and yet has the potential to yield really huge results with relatively small investments of money, or energy

or time even. I think there should be a lot more of it.
I don't think that inherently says that you shouldn't
do the other stuff. I think at its best you have a
synergy between the long-term planning process, and
the short-term possibilities that create momentum
and enthusiasm.

RH: This small-scale approach seems very much in
tune with the reality of how creativity is fostered.
It runs counter to the rhetoric of the 'creative class'
stuff for instance, where creativity is marketed as a
form of economic development.

MW: I think there is an awful lot of bullshit in that
creative class talk; it's not all bullshit, but, you
know...

RH: You met Richard Florida in Canada didn't you?

MW: Yeah, he was a nice guy, good to talk to, we had
an interesting discussion, and there's a common set
of ideas between what he's saying and what I'm
saying. However, there's a totally diametrically
different point from which you view those ideas. The
problem that I get from reading Richard Florida's stuff
is that there's a kind of top-heavy process around a
global creative class, which moves from place to place
seeking a quality of lifestyle or iconic architect-
designed arts centres, you know. That's bloody useless in Newcastle.

It may be relevant for a handful of global cities, or
cities with deep pockets, and it might be slightly relevant for cities which have some desire to develop
some kind of advantage over similar neighbouring
cities, but it's basically irrelevant in Newcastle.
There is no money to spend, there is no global class
that's about to drop there and make it their home. My

starting point is not creativity as something which comes from outside, it's the creativity already latent in the community which we need to manifest.

Some of the arguments do apply, like about creative places being more desirable. I'm not afraid of saying that, but it's a different point. I was challenged at a talk I gave in New York, I was asked how I felt about all these artists coming in from outside and displacing the community. The artists in Newcastle *are* the community. That's the difference. It's not about bringing in a generic idea of what art or culture is, it's about creating a mechanism where the semi-retired ladies who make hats, can make hats. That to me is a much more genuine manifestation of what makes places interesting, desirable, diverse and unique. And it's not divorced from economic development.

THE
NEW
AMSTERD
AM
SCHOOL
DUS
Architects

On the bridge in front of the Lyceum School in Amsterdam's south, there are a pair of sculptures. One depicts a woman with her arm around the shoulder of a young girl, holding a bunch of flowers, with a dove at her feet. The other is of a man with a solid face and a young boy at his knee, holding an engine part. Together they represent the passing down of the values of nature and peace, hard work and industry, to the next generation. Created by sculptor Hildo Krop in 1927, they are examples of the progressive design movement of the early 20th century known as the Amsterdam School.

Although largely defined by its expressionist brickwork and integrated ornament, the Amsterdam School was as much a social movement as an aesthetic one. Holland at the turn of the 20th century was undergoing drastic upheaval. A crisis in agriculture and the rise of industrialisation led to mass internal migration to the cities in search of employment. Property speculators threw up jerry-built tenements; overcrowded and rife with disease. The Housing Act of 1901 sought to rectify these problems by instituting controls on housing standards, principles which were enacted on a grand scale following World War I in 1914, when the Amsterdam School artists and architects created urban spaces of enlightened generosity.

Established in 2004 by Hedwig Heinsman, Hans Vermeulen and Martine de Wit, DUS Architects identify with the Amsterdam School. As the economic crisis reveals the deep inequalities in our societies and exposes our architecture to have neglected its public responsibility, DUS suggest we may be at a similar *fin de siecle* moment 100 years later. While stylistically they could not be further apart, DUS' particular brand of social design and collaborative engagement returns to architecture the principles of civic quality that characterised the movement. Each of their projects – urban renewal, masterplan, interior fitout, new build, product design or party – is approached as an opportunity to create a more social experience, as well as something beautiful.

The Bucky Bar, a temporary pavilion in Rotterdam created out of standard red umbrellas, created a spontaneous street party on a rainy Friday night, drawing hundreds of people out of the cold. The Gecekondu Summerhouse, an illegal travelling hotel with associated events, was named 'best architecture project of the year' by the Dutch newspaper *NRC Handelsblad*.

Both projects illustrate how even the most light-weight spatial construct can lead to a memorable social outcome.

And like the proponents of the Amsterdam School, DUS are not alone. They've recently founded the Open Coop, a shared public work-space which brings various disciplines from design, engineering and performance together under one roof with an active public program. To follow this Amsterdam School precedent right through, today is our 1914; the financial crisis is beginning to subside, and

With a table dividing the space in two, guests need help from the other side if they want both food and drink.

what might be created in its wake is only just becoming apparent. There are exciting times ahead, watch this space...

Conducted 25th November 2011 at the offices of DUS in Amsterdam.

Rory Hyde: I want to start off with a quote from your Momentary Manifesto: 'Number one: architecture by doing is architectural beta-testing'. What do you mean by this, and what's so important about 'doing' for you as a collective?

> Hans Vermeulen: We're really referring to online beta-testing, where you put your ideas into the world without them being totally perfect and ready, and

then learn from the users. It's a sort of reverse research and development process.

Hedwig Heinsman: And it has the double advantage of creating community commitment, engagement and response to it, and you can immediately learn from these reactions to take it further. It's a growing architecture.

RH: This approach would seem to work best on the small-scale social scenarios that you produce – the parties, the pavilions, etc. Are you also interested in doing big public buildings, and can you apply the lessons you learn at this scale?

HH: We think these things need to coexist. It's very interesting to have these temporary happenings and events, but at the same time there is always a need for permanent architecture. It's about the interplay of the two. And that's actually what we're doing here in our new Open Coop office – we are transforming an existing building into a partly public place in which we've already started hosting all sorts of other activities. It's really important to be able to facilitate public platforms for people to meet, as lots can come out of these spontaneous encounters.

HV: And maybe there's not such a big difference between the temporary architecture we can build with our own hands and the bigger public buildings we are building and are going to be building in the future. We want to challenge this idea that a building is a fixed thing; architecture is always constantly changing, and the program and the building are totally interrelated in changing each other.

RH: This also refers to this term you use to describe what you do: 'public architecture'. Immediately you think of libraries, schools, sports pavilions, but your take on it seems to be less about building types and more about public engagement.

HH: The reason we use the word 'public' is because we believe every architect has a public responsibility. But because of the very centralised way housing is procured in Holland, for example, this engagement with the public has largely been lost. The developer or housing corporation is a filter between the people and the architects, which makes the process very complex. But we would like to communicate with the people who will live in our buildings, so we developed what we call the 'DUS method', which is a way of communicating with and learning from the future owners.

RH: I was reading an interview with Bart Lootsma this morning, and he was talking about the contradiction between the very liberal, tolerant, free values of Holland and the very centralised and highly regulated approach to architecture.[34]

HH: Yes, in our attempt to make everything so well-organised, there has developed a kind of democratic dictatorship. There are so many regulations and bureaucracy that in the end there is very little freedom. We do have the feeling that there is a kind of paradigm shift happening right now, and it's an exciting time to be working. When we started our office in 2004 – when Bart Lootsma was talking about Super Dutch – this wasn't the case.[35] We were just graduating, and thinking 'Do we want to become these *Vinex** architects who just decide what sort of facade the building will have?' No, we really wanted to talk about the

* *Vinex* is a national policy document outlining principles for the construction of new residential areas in Holland. While considered a success, it is also deemed to have led to very formulaic design.

program and whether a building should be there at

all. So we started to research, form some alliances with the housing corporations, and through these participatory projects we started to understand their idiom and really make our own kind of architecture.

RH: To follow on with this idea of freedom vs. regulation, you're also interested in this idea of 'gecekondu', the Turkish planning loophole, of sorts, which permits that houses erected in one night can legally stay.

Gecekondu Summerhouse installed on a pontoon at ARCAM, Amsterdam. The structure hosted various debates and events in locations around the city throughout the summer of 2009.

HV: Gecekondu is about simple rules and conditions which, when you let them run, can produce extremely complex outcomes. And that's totally what's lacking in the top-down model here in Holland, where you have one architect or one urbanist planning an entire area. So we talk about *playing* the city instead of *planning* the city; playing with the rules to create different outcomes.

We tested this on a small scale with the Gecekondu Summerhouse, and we noticed there are a lot of people who would love to make a more visible and physical contribution to the public domain, but they don't know that they can, or they don't feel they're allowed. By making an intervention as an architect, it can open up that part of your mind. We noticed when we built this simple space, that it wasn't us who created it, but really the people who started to organise all kinds of things that we never anticipated, like outdoor cinema events, children's parties, self-built swimming pools, urban gardening, lectures, music performances etc. You just have to give people an incentive, a vehicle, and then they will really create something new.

And if we're talking about the role of the architect, there is a need for a mediator, somebody to give a template for change. That sounds cheesy, but if you can facilitate a building or device or whatever, then people can build upon it and make it their own.

RH: The latest example of this is perhaps the Occupy movement. In a way it might be a version of your own theories taking shape in an unexpected way. You talk about a more spontaneous use of the city, of different occupations and additions – then this movement comes along which seems to be doing all these things. Do you see it as an exciting contribution?

HV: It's totally exciting. They have a new kind of language for communication and organisation, which is interesting. But the really good thing about Occupy is that they *do it*. And because they actually do it, every layer of society is talking about it, and that is quite a contribution to the debate. As a generation coming from wealth where everything only went up, we have to get used to taking a stand. And that only happens in the public domain.

HH: Yes, it's interesting to see how the idea of the public cause and the public domain seem completely related. The idea of a public cause has really diminished over the last decades, it has become more and more diffuse, but now it's really taking shape again and reshaping the public. We've been talking a lot about the Amsterdam School of one hundred years ago; at that time, living conditions were poor, and the public really invested in a beautiful public domain that was really important for the well-being of society.

There was a very strong sense of the public cause –
artists, architects, politicians – everyone collaborated,
and now I feel we are again headed towards this.

RH: This perhaps raises the question of your
aesthetic. The Amsterdam School was as much an
aesthetic movement as it was a social movement;
in a way, we can't separate the two. How does your
attitude to the social play out in your aesthetic?

HV: It's totally connected. And I think it relates back
to the Occupy movement: when it doesn't look 'good',

it becomes a problem. In the
end they just look like old
squatters, and people are
afraid. It's about communication. The Bucky Bar was
an 'occupy'; we occupied the
street with an umbrella
dome, and it looked so nice
that nobody thought it was
threatening.

Bucky Bar, a one-night-only unsolicited installation
in Rotterdam which turned into a party.

HH: The police drove past several times, but we didn't
have any trouble.

RH: So the aesthetic is important in engaging the
public by making it more approachable. One of the
other points in your manifesto is to 'avoid authorship';
is this part of the same strategy perhaps? By making
things familiar or almost generic, do they become
more inviting? The Bucky Bar seems to work on this
level.

HH: It almost looks like you could have designed
it yourself. On the one hand we don't want to impose
our grand architecture on people, but at the same
time we do want to trigger them in a certain way. It's

not that we're against a signature or authorship as such, but we want to invite people to make it their own.

HV: And that's what open design is about, having a good designer giving some shape to the world, and the world can do whatever they want with it, even make it better.

RH: Just to shift gears a little, I'm interested in this idea that you didn't come from 'proper' offices. As I understand it, the practice grew naturally out of the work you did together at university rather than from an apprenticeship in an office. How do you think that has shaped the way you work now? Do you seek to emulate other practices or are you more interested in intuitively carving out your own space?

HH: I think it's a question that all three of us feel differently about. I don't want to use the word 'naive', because I don't think it's true... We all worked in offices while we were studying, and so we have some experience there, but in a way our naivety really worked out for us. We dared to ask questions where other people perhaps wouldn't have.

HV: I also think it helps not to be within a framework of what architecture is or should be. We can reinvent architecture because we don't have the burden of the 'right' way to do it. And in another sense it's also nonsense because we went to architecture school, so we are conditioned in that way.

RH: What I find interesting about the kind of practice you have created is that there doesn't seem to be a distinction between the 'real' projects and the 'fun stuff' like the parties or pop-up pavilions that most offices would just do in their spare time.

HH: In a way it's a reaction against the way these other offices work. I didn't want to work like that.

HV: So much architecture is just about choosing the brick colour for a thirty centimetre facade, and for us that's totally not what architecture is.

Martine de Wit: It was really that we wanted to build for people, not for an Excel sheet.

RH: This is a point that has come up in a number of the interviews, particularly from the non-architects. If your aim is to work with people and at the scale of the city, then architecture may not be the answer.

HV: It's one part of it, and it's an interesting part because you can really make beautiful things, but it's not the only thing.

HH: I think our core objective is not working with people, our core objective is making beautiful architecture that hopefully people enjoy. But to do that it's important to engage with the audience you are working with and to acknowledge your social responsibility.

MdW: And by working for people we thought we could make more beautiful things.

RH: But as you mentioned, in the Dutch system there is this restrictive filter between the owner and the architect. How are you able to get around this constraint and work in this more direct way?

HV: The *Vinex* model was really well organised, it was a total production machine, but the people who built them never became the owners, they just sold them on. Build and sell, hit and run. And now we're in this dire situation we're in.

HH: But the great thing about now is that these large developers are looking for new niche markets, to build for specific groups with specific wishes. Groups of people are really starting to get together and demand something better than what the market has to offer.

RH: So you're talking about ten families getting together to build a collective block?

HH: That's what we're moving towards, a pluri-form collective architecture, made up of a vast variety of different small collectives. Which actually brings us back to the Amsterdam School and the cooperative way of building housing. Groups of people who couldn't afford to build their own home would unite in large cooperatives as a way to finance building.

RH: I think that's what's really interesting about the Amsterdam School: these huge developments were all financed privately. And although they were informed by the progressive principles of the welfare state, the housing corporations were all begun as private companies providing a social good.

HV: And that's why it's a really interesting model for today, because the state doesn't have any money anymore, but we have billions of euros in personal savings accounts. We have to organise all this small money, push it together and start building.

DUS Architects

THE PROFESSIONAL GENERALIST

Jeanne Gang

Studio Gang

'Make no little plans. They have no magic to stir men's blood and probably will not themselves be realized'.

This appeal to large-scale ambition by Daniel Burnham, architect and author of the 1909 Plan of Chicago, precisely encapsulates the arrogance of the 19th-century industrial era; a time of untempered faith in the power of infrastructure and technology to shape the environment for the needs of humans alone. Nowhere was this more apparent than Chicago, where in the 1890s a series of canals were dug in a massive undertaking to reverse the direction of the Chicago River and redirect it across the Subcontinental Divide to flow into the Mississippi. While this solved the immediate health crisis by diverting Chicago's sewerage away from its water supply in Lake Michigan, like the old woman who swallowed a fly, it would set off a chain of legal, political and ecological crises, culminating in the con-

Canals built in 1900 across the Subcontinental Divide reversed the flow of the Chicago River and linked ecologically distinct watersheds.

temporary arrival of Asian carp, an invasive species that is radically disrupting the natural balance. This large plan has had large consequences.

The recent publication of *Reverse Effect* by Jeanne Gang explores strategies to rectify these inherited issues of Chicago's waterways, and presents what Gang describes as 'a new approach to urbanism, one that considers the city as an interconnected, ecological system'.[36] The book features proposals by Studio Gang and Gang's students at Harvard, which use the proposed construction of a water barrier as an opportunity to introduce water-cleansing wetlands, green-power stations, permaculture farms and new public spaces. They do not attempt to return the area to its pre-industrial 'natural' state, but to 'support the well-being of the built environment, land, water, and all of their combined inhabitants – from humans all the way down the food chain to algae'.

To shape the environment for the needs of humans alone requires the iron will and unflinching hand of the engineer; the aims are clearly defined, and the means are pragmatic. But to support the needs of an entire ecosystem of plants and animals requires the expertise and knowledge of a diverse array of specialists and stakeholders. To harness the capacity of this disparate experience requires a new kind of integrative thinker: the professional generalist, who has enough general knowledge to know what specialist disciplines to engage, the skills of communication to extract their expertise, the ability to identify the value in this niche knowledge as relevant to the task, and the extraordinary capacity to synthesise it into an integrated whole. This is the new role we need for today, especially as we seek to roll back the damage wrought by centuries of exploitation of our natural systems. Burnham's appeal to 'make no little plans' still stands, but what has changed is who and what we make these plans for, and the skills required to deliver them.

Conducted 28th August 2011 at the Aalto Meeting on Modern Architecture, Jyväskylä, Finland.

Rory Hyde: Your work extends beyond the boundaries of what we might consider the 'native' knowledge or expertise of an architect, to engage various different specialists from different disciplinary backgrounds. Who are the new kinds of people that you find yourself working with?

Jeanne Gang: It really depends on the issues that come up uniquely with each project, but it's the type of project that we're going after that tends to bring them up. Water is an important issue, so hydrologists and civil engineers who deal specifically with water are the ones we seek out. There are unique aspects to water quality which have to do with pathogens and invasive species; therefore you need ecologists and scientists, and then suddenly you find yourself working with – or against – the Army Corps of Engineers, because they maintain control over the waterways in the United States. It is surprising that important decisions regarding ecology are decided by a branch of the military – the Army! – and you think, 'Well, what does the Army have to do with looking after water?', but they're the ones in charge of it. So it's kind of a misfit, and I think that's one of the challenges when you're dealing with waterways, cities and green infrastructure, because it's not a group of people who are sympathetic to the things that we're talking about; they're trying to protect those spaces from a military standpoint.

RH: So what is your role in these situations? Do you act as an integrator or translator between these different groups with wildly different sets of expertise and interests?

JG: Yes, absolutely, because as architects we're kind of generalists – we know a little bit about a lot of things – so we sometimes end up being the translator or integrator. Also, it becomes about which persons you put in the same room together. Under the old way, it used to be that you would just meet with each consultant individually, but the amazing thing is that when you have them all in the same room together, it is possible to tease the ideas out of the group.

So, for example, in the Lincoln Park Zoo project, the brief was not to create green infrastructure. The client asked us for an aesthetic improvement of the site, but because we had everyone there collaborating from the beginning, we found that instead of just

The Professional Generalist

replacing the concrete edge around the pond, we could literally pull it out and replace it with flora to improve the water quality. We could improve the habitat by deepening the pond to allow fish to winter over, and to allow for proper oxygenation of the water; those were all things that came up at the very beginning through collaboration. We were able to use the dirt that we pulled out to create some mounds for play areas and things like that in the landscape as

A 'blue-green future' for Chicago. Renewed waterways culminate in a series of freshwater inland lagoons, around which 'an attractive urban fabric will grow'.

well. So these ideas wouldn't happen unless you had all the experts in the same room at the same time, and the architect is usually the one who knows which people should be there and gets them in the same place.

RH: In your presentation you showed these incredible historical photos of the highly exploitative approach to the landscape of the 19th century. These types of projects sound very specific to the Chicago context, but also to post-industrial cities in general.

JG: Right, it's not just Chicago, but any city that developed their infrastructure in the early 20th century. Back then, the idea was that we could overpower anything; that we could design a pipe big enough to hold the water when there's a flood – but today you can't anymore, because the climate is changing, so it becomes more and more expensive, and we don't have the same kind of resources today to build massive infrastructure projects in America. So the green infrastructure projects are partly a solution to the grey and decaying infrastructure that we inherited. What I mean is that implementing green infrastructure is not just about being ecologically correct, it's also about literally solving some of these problems in a much cheaper way – which fortunately has the added benefit of making the space nicer for people.

RH: You mentioned a fascinating anecdote about the limestone in Kentucky which makes the grass grow in a certain way which leads to the fantastic racehorses that this place is known for. It seems like an apt metaphor for your approach to architecture as part of a larger system. Is there any edge to architecture, or do we need to just keep on looking?

JG: That story is a fabulous example of how something that comes authentically from a place influences what that place becomes known for – raising racehorses with strong bones, because of the geology! It makes sense, but who would have thought of that?! But, maybe it has to do with our generation and the next generation of architects having many more tools at our disposal. It's like a magnifying glass; once you look through it you suddenly see all these details that you didn't see were there before. So that's a little bit like what's happening in architecture, because suddenly we can see all these relationships, new relationships, causalities, with a finer grain than we've been able to observe in the past. It's really like the new frontier for architecture in my view; we just have so much more access to a depth of information that wasn't visible before.

RH: Speaking of magnifying glasses, one of the other interesting aspects to your presentation was the use of new kinds of imagery. We saw this Doppler radar image of bird migration, a map of the larger-scale migratory patterns across the Americas, magnified images of bone structures and coral. How you see this relationship between the very technical and the very human at the other end of the scale?

JG: Research is usually the way that we begin a project, and sometimes the research is scattershot – 'let's look into this because it seems like it might be a productive thing', or 'let's look into that' – it's not that you necessarily know what the results of the research are going to bring, and so when you discover something interesting that you know is worth pursuing, that's when it becomes exciting. Also, I think the other part of it is that you can't just keep researching forever; you have to be able to turn it off and make things, in order to let the research that has sunk into your brain and into everyone on the team's brains take shape – just stop the research now, and let's produce something. What's interesting is that a lot of times research reveals itself in the thing that you make. I really think it's important to let there be a creative period in the project and not let the research dictate what it's going to be. We come to form at a later stage after we've done the research, instead of starting and saying 'Oh, what kind of cool form can we make?', which is a way some others start. They might produce a form they like and then analyse and make it more performative later. So I guess we reverse that by starting more analytically, and then kind of cutting loose at some point.

RH: You also mentioned that you are teaching studios at Harvard and also at the Illinois Institute of Technology. How does that research with the students feed back into the office? How does that relationship develop?

JG: For me, I like working with students and collaborating with students because you can add more diversity to the problems, but it's also a chance to put a problem out there that's not necessarily a commission. Because if we have a commission for a project, we're already doing the research in-house – we have a lab already within our office – but if the research is for an issue that doesn't readily fit with projects already underway, it's great to collaborate with students and to speculate. I see it as the same process in the office or in the academy: we all learn about an issue together – I come to it with the same approach, bringing in different experts – and then there's a jumping-off point when the student then takes it into his or her more individual domain. So, the academy provides a venue to work with others, but the subject matter might be something we have not had the opportunity to explore in the office.

RH: Another key theme in your work is to address the needs beyond just those of people, to include and encourage diverse species of animals and plants in your proposals. Can architectural form be used to promote biodiversity?

JG: Well, yes, it can. Mass urbanisation, which is already very familiar territory for architects and urbanists, also has an impact on other species. I think we need to ensure we pay attention to biodiversity. And that's not just 'OK, let's save the cute little animals', it's really the key to our own survival too, because we haven't yet discovered precisely what's needed to continue to support our healthy ecosystem that humans are a part of. So with some of our projects we've taken this on and we're really crossing over into making environments that are attractive to wildlife – animals and plants – in addition to people, to preserve biodiversity. So, for example, with the Lincoln Park Zoo project, we're really amping up and exaggerating the habitats, making the site super attractive to the animals, and then it's also an incredibly public space, so how do these two things interconnect?

I was at the site recently and saw a coyote – this is right in the downtown area, and they're usually very shy. There are over two thousand coyotes in the Chicago region, but they're very hard to spot. In this public space at the Lincoln Park Zoo, it just felt right at home and it showed itself. So that was kind of amazing and some would say problematic. But perhaps there is a way to coexist. It certainly begins to build awareness that was otherwise not there. Also, with the zoo, we worked on creating attractive habitats, you know, putting dead, rotting logs in places that a typical landscape designer might think were unsightly. But from a biodiversity perspective, these supposedly ugly things can play another role. I actually don't think they are ugly. You see a lot of landscape architects designing monocultures for purely aesthetic reasons, but these are not that great at attracting living things. I'd like to see our profession expanding the aesthetic palette in the landscape with a better understanding of the ecological function – it may look very different than what we are accustomed to, which is exciting. We don't necessarily have to be interested in replicating how nature looks, but we should understand how it functions and how it works.

With the Ford Calumet project, we asked ourselves 'What if the building was more like a nest?' The ecological system that we're exploring there is the idea of closed loops and re-use by designing a building that employs materials and salvage that is available, abundant and nearby. We designed the structural system for the building by asking our engineers to think about different sizes of steel sections that would work as columns, so there's this kind of built-in flexibility geared toward what will be available at the time of construction, instead of specifying the precise shape in advance. So when the time comes to get the materials, they could be from different sources, and they would still work. So it's almost like a built-in diversity of column types that reduces the embodied energy and becomes the aesthetic simultaneously.

RH: On the way down here you mentioned that one of the criticisms of the Aqua Tower is that 'it's just an icon', whereas in your presentation we saw the complexity – you called it a 'Gordian knot' – of infrastructure, of background and underground systems that go into a project like this.

JG: I was likening a tall building like Aqua to a piece of infrastructure, rather than a building object, because not only is it connecting multiple levels of the city to roadways, to trains – all of that infrastructure is under the ground – it's also a piece of infrastructure for people. People will be moving in and out of a building this scale, so it has to accommodate and be flexible to hundreds of residents. I see it as a concrete

The Professional Generalist

surface that anyone can plug into and use.

RH: You also presented your project for MoMA's upcoming exhibit Foreclosed. Foreclosure is such a complex issue operating at multiple scales – from national economic policy and local lending practices, to long-term societal transitions – which all come to bear at the scale of an individual family and an individual house. What was your approach to understanding this problem and what kinds of experts did you enlist?

Aqua Tower, mixed-use residential tower in Chicago's Lakeshore East.

JG: For so long, affordable housing in the US has been built by entities that have very little interest in design. But design is precisely what is needed; not just new physical forms, but a way of design that explores new types of ownership and flexibility that are no longer satisfied by the traditional single-family house with a mortgage. I enlisted housing advocates, financial gurus, urban designers, landscape architects, artists and ecologists to address the issue.

RH: Your project focuses on the town of Cicero, Illinois, which you describe as an 'arrival city' as it is the first stop for many immigrant families arriving to the US. You describe your goal as to transform Cicero into a city that takes these arrivals and

'propels them into the middle class'. What are some of
the strategies you have proposed to achieve this?

> JG: First, we realised that for Cicero – an inner-ring
> suburb that saw the foreclosure of its industry in
> recent years – the main issue causing poverty was the
> loss of jobs. Without factories, people would benefit
> from being able to start small entrepreneurial busi-
> nesses and work from home. Living and working
> together with access to shared resources, like car
> sharing, for example, would decrease expenses and
> make things more affordable. The family type has
> also changed and the single-family house no longer
> meets the needs of today's diverse family structures.
> We designed a live–work housing type that allows res-
> idents to expand or contract their space and share
> spaces such as workshops or kitchens, making both
> more affordable and more functional.

RH: You also describe the economic model of this
project; in what ways is it financially viable over a
longer term? Is this a model for how cities or suburbs
might be able to be more resilient in the face of economic downturns in the future?

> JG: Yes, we added a financial model that would sup-
> port this design that would allow people to buy and
> sell shares in the project according to how much they
> need. The land is held in a trust so that the value of
> homes can increase with sweat equity, but the value
> of the real estate would avoid the wild swings that we
> saw in the economic downturn.

THE ARCHITECT

AS PUBLIC INTELLECTUAL

Conrad Hamann on

Robin Boyd

The definition of a public intellectual is a highly contested one, ranging from Richard Posner's uselessly polite 'intellectuals who opine to an educated public on questions of ... political or ideological concern', to Edward Said's disruptive activist 'scoffer whose place it is publicly to raise embarrassing questions'. More constructively, Christopher Hitchens offers a criteria of perception that a public intellectual ought to hold, including 'the ability to survey the present through the optic of a historian, the past with the perspective of the living, and the culture and language of others with the equipment of an internationalist'.

With a command of history, a capacity for astute cultural interpretation, an ability to imagine futures beyond the immediate and the communicative skill to present these possibilities in a compelling manner, architects ought to be well positioned for this role. And yet our contemporary public intellectuals typically come from the fields of literature, science, journalism or politics. In *Prospect Magazine*'s most recent poll of the top 100 public intellectuals, only Rem Koolhaas made the grade at number 88. With his background in journalism, opining on topics as diverse as shopping, the European Union, Lagos,

Conrad Hamann

Dubai and China, and his prolific output of books, Koolhaas is perhaps the exception that proves the rule.

In order to be a public intellectual, one must be able to stick one's head above the parapet, to ask the tough questions and challenge the status quo. As a profession dependent upon the commissions of governments and corporations, such necessary outspokenness could be viewed as a conflict of interest.

Robin Boyd (1919–1971), Australian architect and outspoken social commentator, offers a lesser-known precedent for the architect as public intellectual. Combining a sharp wit and a compelling presence with a strong sense of civic duty, Boyd employed all facets of the media in his campaign to shape the cultural debate of Australia and beyond. His best-known work is *The Australian Ugliness* (1960), which, as the title suggests, is a scathing attack on what Boyd saw to be the dismal state of the Australian urban environment. And yet despite the elitism of this critique,

Drawing by Boyd for the cover of *The Australian Ugliness*, a desolate suburban landscape of garish signage, telephone poles and over-pruned trees.

it would become a national bestseller, capturing an audience far beyond the insular world of architecture.

A more constructive response to this issue was the Small Homes Service, a revolutionary program which created simple, innovative and modern house plans for sale for only £5 each, which were then advertised through Boyd's column in Melbourne's *The Age* newspaper, changing the shape of the suburbs for the better.

As our urban environments continue to face the pressure of private interests and public short-sightedness, this is a critical role for today. With a sophisticated understanding of the interface between spatial concerns and the larger forces of politics and cultural trends, the architect as public intellectual has the capacity to imagine potential spatial futures that are foremost in the public's interest. This interview with historian of Australian architecture and Boyd expert Dr Conrad Hamann explores Boyd's diverse exploits in the public sphere, and reflects on the challenges facing the adoption of a similar role in today's highly prescriptive intellectual climate.

Conducted 22nd April 2011 at The Mess Hall café in Melbourne.

Rory Hyde: I'm interested in speaking to you in particular about Boyd's different strategies for reaching the public and his use of the media. I see him as a fascinating prototype for an architect as a public figure engaged with civic issues.

Conrad Hamann: He was unusual in that sense. It wasn't as if his arguments or ideas were so original; it was more that he was keen enough and persistent enough as a writer to get it through to a wider audience. If you track his arguments you can find most of them in earlier decades one way or another.

Even the idea for the Small Homes Service had been advanced by George Sydney Jones, who was quite a radical architect in Sydney, to be run out of the NSW Institute of Architects in the 1900s. *Home Beautiful* magazine had a small homes service running in the 1930s. It was in 1947 when *The Age* newspaper and the RVIA, as the institute was known back then, got together and organised a regular column. Boyd, with various notable assistants including Neil Clerehan and Kevin Borland, set up the office in Myers department store and they would produce these home designs and sell them for about five pounds each.

RH: So how did it actually work? They would design a house and Boyd would use the newspaper column to advertise it?

CH: Yes, he would. He would take a design and describe it, and then he'd range around that and discuss an aspect of modern architecture and its contemporary significance, sometimes tying it back to that particular design. When one design had few takers, he re-ran the drawings heading them 'Unpopular

Design!', asking why it was unpopular, and using that as a lever to raise consciousness about the nuances of modern architecture.

RH: Because that really was his campaign: to educate the public in his battle against the traditionalists.

CH: Yes, he was committed to educating people about modern architecture. And it was a propitious time, because World War II had blown away a lot of people's inhibitions about doing something new or radical. A lot of households had at least one returned man or woman in their number, and people had been within an inch of losing their lives, so I think in those early post-war years they were much more willing to experiment. Nowadays, in comparison, you'd have a much smaller constituency for progressive architecture per capita. A lot of councils have even outlawed contemporary buildings; in Altona Meadows, people wanting to build anything other than neo-Federation or neo-Georgian had a very difficult time getting a permit.

RH: Neil Clerehan recently said he'd thought they'd swayed the public against traditionalism in the 1950s and 1960s, only for it to rear its head again in the form of today's McMansions.

CH: Architects were ambushed by the McMansion – rather like the way Labour was blindsided by the emergence of right-wing populism in the 1970s!

RH: I found this nice quote where Boyd asks 'How could architecture ever progress if it was to remain available only to the well-to-do?'[37]

CH: I think that was a crucial issue. Every McMansion that's built is really a by-passing of architectural possibilities in favour of a generic type,

Conrad Hamann

which for various reasons is liked by real-estate agents, probably because it's got a certain amount of decorative character.

RH: As architects, do you think we've abandoned that obligation to educate the public, or do you think we decided that taste isn't important – a bit too culturally imperialistic – and that people should just have what they want?

CH: Yes, I think there was an issue there. Post-modernism certainly involved the revision of attitudes towards modern architecture's mission of raising public taste. So there was probably a reaction at least on that basis. But in the end Australia did not see a whole-hearted pursuit of inclusive architecture either. There's now a lot of neo-Modernism, basically rebels in surface materials, so even that's become a repetitive nostalgic exercise. But yes, I think there was an abdication. Whether or not this was entirely architects' doing is another matter, but certainly since the early 1980s the writing was on the wall for architects' involvement with 'everyday' clients.

One of Boyd's 'Small Homes' columns in *The Age* newspaper, 1951.

RH: According to Serle, by 1951 ten percent of houses on Melbourne's suburban fringe were built to plans by the Small Homes Service, and many more were influenced by it. I can't think of a similarly impactful project on the

212

market at large. Do you think it was the media that gave it that push?

CH: I think it was, and Boyd himself was very keen to use the media strategically. Boyd was anxious to get the word out, and also to get his name known. He was always eagerly involved in media, first with *Smudges*, then in *Plan* which was just about to start up when World War II intervened. He then came back and wrote *Victorian Modern* in 1947, and then went to *The Age*.

Robin Boyd and Neil Clerehan mounting an exhibition of the Small Homes Service, 1953.

RH: What do you think drove him to do all this writing? Was it a civic responsibility or more self-promotion?

CH: It was probably a bit of a mixture: I think he was keen to be well known and also keen to make a mark. Serle notes this in his biography. The Boyd family was already notable in writing, art and pioneering, so perhaps it seemed like a natural step. His mother was a painter, his father had been a painter. It was in the blood. The Boyds had always done interesting or extraordinary things, and there has been a perception that they were bred to it. But there was probably a sense of family and social obligation as well.

His interest in advocating modern architecture seemed to go beyond that of most of his contemporaries. He did seem to have a commitment to 'Architecture', which seemed to carry him at least into the medium of writing, and took him into an area where most architects weren't prepared to go. Not to say that he was a better writer than most; I personally find Boyd a fairly ordinary writer.

RH: But Boyd was funny!

CH: Boyd had an interesting and attentive take on society. He was obviously very observant and keen to write all of that down and record it. Hence *The Australian Ugliness*, which is a Dickensian romp for the first half. After that it gets all sober and prescriptive, but for the first half he takes an almost wicked delight in one grotesquery after another! He saw people's personalities as somehow mirrored in their architectural and physical surroundings.

RH: This focus on personality is interesting because that then lifts his criticism from being simply stylistic to being one about the character of the country.

CH: I think it does; it's not architecture divorced from its society.

RH: There's a great line where he really nails the Australian character he's attacking: 'a vitality, energy, strength, and optimism in one's own ability, yet indolence, carelessness, the "She'll do, mate" attitude to the job to be done'.[38]

CH: Yes, 'near enough is good enough'. And it was reflected in everything from brick veneer to boxed eaves and chopping down trees. The question is whether these things were fundamentally Australian or shared by many others. I do think he tended to over-particularise to Australia, he tended to put forward the idea that Australia was the only place where this or that negative thing could occur. This related particularly to 'tall poppies', when in actual fact you can find tall poppies chopped down busily in every

The Architect as Public Intellectual

country. There's no statistical basis on which Australia's distinctiveness vis-a-vis tall poppies is any worse or in any way outstanding compared to the rest of the world. Think about the famous 'Wilderness' Louis Sullivan and Frank Lloyd Wright found themselves in after 1914, in a country with a far larger population. In contrast Marion and Walter Burley Griffin were able to get about one hundred eighty projects in Australia, of which they built maybe one hundred; Louis Sullivan was lucky to get half a dozen in the same period.

RH: So there was a fairly open-minded attitude, and an interest in self-improvement here.

CH: At certain levels. For instance Boyd talks about and projects a real fellowship that seems to exist among the old diggers, I think he felt optimistic that it was a generation prepared to experiment. At the same time he did become disillusioned by the early 1950s; I think he felt that post-war austerity had stamped out a lot of the little embryonic offices, and that a lot of newly-trained architects had been forced out of architecture altogether. So I think he saw the prolongation of post-war austerity in which Australia was adjusting from a war economy to a civilian economy as basically pushing people back into the arms of project builders and so on, and gaining a foothold for conservative taste.

RH: So that's what justifies this strike which is *The Australian Ugliness*. How was it received? It's hard to imagine someone to be so outspoken today, speaking of tall poppies...

CH: It was really popular. There was an incredibly enthusiastic reaction. The take that people had on *The Australian Ugliness* varied; there were a lot of letters about people getting out and cleaning up litter, and certainly a lot of people got the message about signage. Boyd had a strong argument that garish roadside signage was detracting from the environment, and he argued a shift in attitude toward signage based particularly on Switzerland and Scandinavia. He then argued that America had garish signage, but that was culturally authentic to America, because they'd invented it! [laughs] Which is an argument that I suspect doesn't quite hold up.

The other issue, I suppose, is to what extent is modern architecture about radical social transformation, or to what extent is it about the improvement of taste? Boyd was well aware that taste is a trap – he writes about that in *Victorian Modern* – but in later years I think he has an ambivalent position in his engagement to modern architecture as to whether it's an issue about improving taste, or whether it's got something more radical behind it. And I don't think he ever ultimately resolves that conflict.

RH: Beyond the books, Boyd also used other media such as television and radio to spread his message, as well as the international journals.

CH: I haven't surveyed his TV output thoroughly, but I certainly know his series *Design in Australia*. And then there was the *Boyer Lectures* which was on radio, which became the book *Artificial Australia*. He also made the film *Your House and Mine* with Peter MacIntyre. He actually covered a very broad spectrum of media in that sense. He wrote for *Meanjin*, he wrote an entry for the *Encyclopaedia Britannica* on Australian housing, he of course also wrote regularly for *Architectural Forum* and the *Architectural Review* in London, for the *Architectural Record* and *Progressive*

Architecture in the US, plus *L'Architecture d'Aujourd'hui* in France, *Casabella* and *Domus* in Italy, and so on. He had a very broad array of media coverage and engagements, but I think writing was the primary instrument and radio and visual media was a kind of offshoot from it.

RH: That's one of the most impressive things to me looking back: that in the days of snail mail, and before real international travel, he could build these bonds with the greats in America and in Europe, teach at MIT, make friends with Walter Gropius, and even put together one of the first books in English on Japanese architect Kenzo Tange.[39]

Walter Gropius (second from left) on a trip to Victoria with Robin Boyd (right), 1954.

CH: That's right, and all of that was done by Super Constellation or DC-4! [laughs]

RH: How did he develop such an international outlook?

CH: He was very keen to develop architecture on an international stage, he was incredibly dogged and determined. I think the Haddon Travelling Scholarship [awarded in 1948] was really important, and he made that post a winner by making contact with Nicolaus Pevsner, Reyner Banham and Jim Richards – the trifecta on the London *Architectural Review*. They were the ones you really zeroed in on.

Vincent Scully, whom I talked to about this, had met Robin Boyd and knew him. And Manfredo Tafuri also shows a great awareness of Boyd in his *Theories and History of Architecture* published in 1980. He uses

Boyd quite a bit, but clearly Boyd was coming from a theoretical framework that was outside of Tafuri's...

RH: And did any of this writing pay off in the form of commissions?

CH: That was very much a mixture. He got a wave of residential commissions, mostly from clients of fairly moderate means, in the wake of the Small Homes articles. They said they liked the Small Homes designs but that they would like something a bit different or customised. So in 1955 alone there were twenty house projects on the go from his side of the office.

RH: It was also one of his big regrets not to have worked on larger projects, something which his media profile may not have helped, as you weren't allowed to publicly spruik for work as a member of the Institute back then.

CH: I think he found himself as a sort of 'Prometheus bound' figure: here he was with his Melbourne Club membership, invited onto committees here, there and everywhere, awarded a CBE [Commander of the British Empire] which he said was a 'useless bauble' as it never seemed to attract more work.

RH: Gideon Haigh recounts an anecdote where businessmen would approach him and say 'You're an architect, who should I get to do my office?'[40] And he's too polite to say 'Me!'

CH: Someone who was a bit more street-smart in that circumstance would have gone for the jugular.

RH: It must have been confusing though; while all the writing must have put his name out there, it may have diluted his status as a 'real architect'. How did

his partners Roy Grounds and Frederick Romberg
view the amount of attention he gave to the writing?

CH: Grounds was particularly impatient, while Romberg was fairly even-handed. According to Romberg, Grounds would say 'You're a scribbler Robby, and you need to make up your mind: are you an architect or are you just interested in dabbling in articles here and there?' Grounds was of the opinion that the presence or otherwise of articles didn't make one iota of difference to the prosperity of the office, which was Grounds' priority. And you could probably say the same about the presence or otherwise of public honours: they don't necessary translate into commissions.

Now for Boyd the real problem was that precisely the moment he wanted to get into these big commercial and institutional works in 1961, Roy Grounds was splitting off from the office, taking the Arts Centre and a number of bigger clients with him. Then came the credit squeeze, and I think Robin just survived on what was left over, while Romberg saw the writing on the wall and took up a teaching post in Newcastle.

RH: He did have a number of larger commissions of course, but they're regarded as less successful than the houses.

CH: These larger projects brought with them problems of project administration, and just Murphy's Law, that really stressed him out of his mind. There were a lot of difficulties at Menzies College, for example, about leaks and problems with the day-to-day management of the project.

RH: Was he interested in that? Or was he only interested in the big idea?

Conrad Hamann

CH: He was really focused on the big idea. There had been difficulties with the houses as well. At one stage Boyd wrote back from the US where he'd been getting all these letters from the office with questions about what to do with such and such a house, how to fix this detail, the chimney's smoking again, etc. and he says he's having nightmares of clients standing around his bed all shaking their heads disapprovingly and then disappearing in clouds of smoke!

RH: [laughs] His role as a wit, a commentator, even a 'public intellectual' seemed to fit him much better.

CH: That's right. I was thinking about this idea of the public intellectual, and Boyd seems to assume that role at around the same time that others are also starting to assume a similar position: Manning Clark as a historian who gave Australian history a public and poetic countenance, or A.A. Phillips who was very much a public face for literature. All these people took Australia's culture into a wider sphere.

RH: Do we have any figures who might be comparable today?

CH: I think the problem now, and it's quite a significant issue, is that the publications and the Australian-British publication criteria for academic promotion actively discourage the public intellectual. If you want credit for writing you have to have it in a refereed journal. It's now reached almost obsessive levels where periodicals are being graded in such a way where people are discouraged from writing for either new journals or ones with a wide public application. If you want to get your message out to more people, you're much better off writing for the commercial magazines.

RH: And you're also not constrained by the strictures of academic writing; you can afford to be a bit more playful in the same way that Boyd was.

CH: Yes, he had a flexibility which is now becoming increasingly illusive for academics who are held to account by the degree to which they satisfy increasingly narrow criteria. I think the implication is that if you want to be a public intellectual, you have to operate outside of – funnily enough – the universities and their publishing systems.

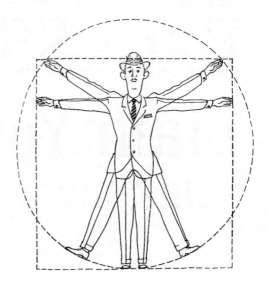

'The pursuit of pleasingness', illustration by Boyd from *The Australian Ugliness*.

Conrad Hamann

THE
EDUCATOR
OF
EXCESS

Liam Young
Unknown Fields

'Beyond the treeline and without the sun for a week. Stuck in the plot for 30 Days of Night. *Can't get a flight out of Barrow AK'* — *@liam_young*

As I'm writing this, Liam Young's Twitter feed offers an update on his latest trip to the remote wilderness with the Architecture Association's (AA) Unknown Fields Division, and it doesn't sound good. He's taken a dozen architecture students into far north Alaska in the dead of winter on an exploration of the cultural, military, technological and ecological fictions and realities that play out in this terrain, and it now appears they're stranded.

But why would architects go there at all? As Young explains, 'we can watch a discussion of climate change on the BBC, and we can examine it through data, or we can go out there and see the glaciers melting, the snow turning yellow from acid rain, and the impacts of these changes on the Inuit populations and their hunting practices. Travelling to these sites allows us to see the real effects on culture and ways of life'.

The idea of architects exploring the world beyond their immediate surrounds has a long and distinguished history. The 'grand tours' of the 17th and 18th centuries would take groups of students from London across the channel to soak up the sights, languages, geography and architecture of continental Europe. Knowledge of architectural styles and history had been widely disseminated through books since the 15th century, but it held that it was only through direct experience that a deeper understanding and impression could be gained. These impressions found their way back across the channel in the UK's proud legacy of Palladian, Baroque and Romanesque influences in its architecture.

With that in mind, what might be the deeper impressions picked up on Young's Unknown Fields expeditions? An acute sensitivity and understanding of the causes and symptoms of climate change would seem to be a profoundly useful trait for a young graduate architect today. There may not be a particular job waiting, but Young seems far less interested in producing fodder for design studios as they currently exist, rather than producing creative and strategic thinkers able to synthesise the challenges of the future.

Unlike the grand tours, these excursions into Unknown Fields are unlikely to produce an equivalent legacy of buildings, as the students find themselves working in such diverse careers as film and television, research, art and

The Educator of Excess

journalism. But perhaps it is precisely this diversity that points to the architectural legacy of these contemporary grand tours, a legacy in the larger and more pressing project of redefining the boundaries of the discipline itself. If they ever make it back, that is…

Conducted 5th December 2011 over Skype between Amsterdam and London.

Rory Hyde: I'm going to start with this incredible statement you made: 'architects' skills are wasted on buildings'. On the one hand it's ridiculous – what else did I study for all those years? – but I also strangely find myself agreeing with it; it highlights the mismatch between the kind of conceptual thinking exercised by architects and the banal reality of bringing buildings into the world. The question is, if our skills are wasted on buildings, where else could we better deploy them?

Liam Young: The answer to that question will come up again and again throughout our conversation. It's why we formed a think-tank instead of a traditional architectural office, it's why we run the Unknown Fields teaching studio the way that we do, but the core of it is that as architects we exist at this extraordinary intersection between the cultural and the technological. Our skill sets involve the synthesis of quite complex and contradictory elements – social, technical, cultural, political and environmental scenarios – which we draw from to propose alternative scenarios. I think that this broad base and understanding is wasted on making buildings as singular objects; there are far more ways that we can be active in the

Liam Young

Overleaf: the Unknown Fields division explores the vanishing Arctic ice cap.

processes that actually shape the world. To put all our eggs in the building basket seems ridiculous.

RH: It also feels like the world has changed yet architecture has failed to adapt, and that might be the space you are exploring. When everyone has a phone in their pocket that can tap into an invisible cloud of swarming data, when our friends are virtualised and our plants tweet us when they need water, it's a fundamentally different space of operation. What do we do as architects when the dominant building materials exist outside of the physical spectrum?

LY: I do believe these changes force us to rethink what the very core of our profession is. There will always be physical objects and spaces that need some architect-like character to engage with it, but this zone of operation will become increasingly narrow. To continue to define our work within this part of the spectrum will just lead us to become further marginalised, irrelevant and ineffective. Cities are now being planned around the speed of electrons and satellite sight lines; connection to wifi is more critical than the old urbanist ideals of connection to light and air. We are interested in the idea of the architect as software engineer, as infrastructuralist, as media strategist, as some sort of trans-media guru – all of these forms are not departures away from the profession but are about expanding what we think of as being the profession. They expand the umbrella of what we do as architects, as opposed to moving outside of architecture in order to engage in those aspects of the world.

RH: I'm interested in how you are exploring these adjacent territories or various definitions of what an architect can be, in particular through your office with Daryl Chen, Tomorrow's Thoughts Today (TTT), which you describe as a 'think-tank' rather than as a design studio. How does it operate, and what do you produce?

LY: What we wanted to do with TTT was to develop a model of practice which would be able to engage critically with contemporary culture. Architecture is traditionally such a slow medium, and we became frustrated working within that mould; we wanted to expand what the architect could be and identify new types of projects which we could address with more immediacy. The idea of a think-tank enables us to focus on speculation and research as products in themselves. There is a culture within architecture of doing speculative projects but it's always seen as something which leads to some form of built practice, or as some kind of weaker version of it.

Electronic Countermeasures, a series of interactive illuminated swarming drones, performed in Eindhoven.

RH: The real outcome is deferred somehow.

LY: Yes, and we wanted to negate that and explore the research model as an endpoint in itself. For us, TTT is more like a music producer who marshals different people together; we bring in people from science or from technology to build a team depending on the nature of the problem or project, allowing us to be dynamic. It's a kind of 'post-bust' office model that is less connected with the economy of building, but more connected with industry, technology, ecology or development at different times. And instead of operating as a service, producing optimistic views of things to clients in order to get paid, we develop self-initiated projects and operate as a consultancy, which allows us to explore dystopias, unintended consequences and provocations. I think we are in a time where we have to develop more resilient forms of practice and this is our attempt to do so.

Forms of practice tied to the economy of making buildings are always limited in some form. We went through a period in the 1980s where unbuilt projects dominated the discussion, which evolved as the economy started to pick up and most innovative forms of practice occurred within the building industry; the conversation shifts to ideas of surface, materiality and in turn to modes of production and digital computation which allow this new formal exploration and surface articulation. The avant-garde of the profession has always been tied to the economy in ways that it doesn't necessarily need to be. That is part of our thinking with TTT: to break that cycle, and to operate in a more dynamic way with a new business model.

RH: The use of fictional futures and narratives seem to be core to how you view your practice and the work you produce. I've always seen architecture as being inherently about the future, about imagining things that don't yet exist, but the sorts of futures you talk about are different somehow, further afield perhaps.

LY: Yes, the ability to have one foot in a believable reality and one in speculation is what allows a fictional or future project to have its critical edge. The near future is a great space, because at the core we are interested in the role of futures and fiction to pose questions, not just find solutions to problems, but to identify new spaces for operation. They are narrative scenarios, positioned in such a way that the audience

The Educator of Excess

can develop an emotional and critical response to them, rather than just dealing with ideas in an abstract way. It's all about prototyping culture, and prototyping new rules, not predicting the future, because in the end, as Warren Ellis says, 'prediction is always just science fiction's side effect'. So for us the future isn't what happens when we imagine it and make images of it; the future happens when someone reads it, responds to it and wants to start to make it.

RH: One of your other key projects is the Unknown Fields Division you run with Kate Davies at the AA. You explore what you call 'unreal and forgotten land-scapes, alien terrains and obsolete ecologies', taking groups of students to the Galapagos, the gold mines in Australia, Russian space camps, the Chernobyl exclusion zone, and next is far north Alaska. Why might architects be interested in these places?

LY: If TTT is about imagining alternative futures, Unknown Fields is about exploring alternative worlds which exist in the present as a way of understanding the world in a new way. So, far from the metropolis lie these dislocated hinterlands, or we call them remote wildernesses, that support the mechanisation of modern living, existing on the margins of our cultural consciousness. We travel behind the scenes of the cities we are familiar with to see these landscapes which are typically forgotten, or are only seen through a particular media narrative. The interest is not to fetishise them as extraordinary places to go, but from these terrains we are able to look back at our world from outside of it. We look for sights that offer a new perspective by which to understand the emerging conditions we are designing for, landscapes where we find the future in the present tense. That's the key phrase we work with. As Proust says, 'the real voyage of discovery consists not in seeking new landscapes but in having new eyes'.

In order to develop the agenda for each field expedition, we scour the pages of *New Scientist* and news broadcasts; we look to popular culture for urgent issues that as architects and urbanists we can somehow offer a unique position on. We look for sites which seem to be microcosms of the emerging world, that in many ways we can only deal with in an abstract way back in cities like London, New York or Amsterdam. So, these are places which are on the borders of our knowledge but where issues like climate change, depleting resources, declining biodiversity or pervasive technology play out with more immediacy, more urgency, and across a more visible timescale.

A student gathering research in Alaska as part of an Unknown Fields trip.

We travel to Alaska, we see the glaciers melting, we see the impacts of these changes on the Inuit populations and their hunting practices. We can talk about a change in climate and ecology through data, through projective models, or we can go out to these landscapes and talk about it through changes in ways of life, through its real effects on culture. For us as designers they form test beds for us to critically evaluate the implications and consequences of emerging technologies; in these sites we can act with more criticality and more immediacy in a way that's difficult to attain through more traditional architecture.

RH: One of the most potent examples which has come out of this work for me in terms of cultural implications, is your discovery in Australia of this parametric gold mine in a place of incredibly deep cultural significance…

LY: I love that tag line from *Easy Rider* – 'Two men went off in search of America and never found it' – and in a way that's what we found when we went off in search of wilderness; we still haven't found it. We realise there is no new nature anymore, at least as we culturally define what nature really was. In the end what we end up doing is travelling to these places of the 'anthropocenic', we really love this term – landscapes of our own making. They are new sites of the sublime, filled with the wonders and horrors of the modern world, and the example of this landscape in Australia is the most tangible and emotive we have found.

It really is an extraordinary place, understood by the indigenous Australians through a network of stories, a landscape of mythology where the land formations contain the stories of their own creation. Whether it's a rainbow serpent slinking through the landscape to carve a river, or a dog on its back to make a mountain, it's a landscape which is understood through the oral traditions of its indigenous culture. And into this extraordinary context you now have these extraordinary new technologies of *mining* as the landscape is cut to obtain the resources which are the makings of the modern world. You have the gold mines that generate the resources that go into all our bits of technology, because gold is an extraordinary conductor of electricity and is non-corrosive; you

Liam Young

have the iron-ore mines that mine the ore that goes to China to make steel to make cities.

You also have an amazing connection between the technologies we surround ourselves with and the shape of the landscape; a real-time connection between the mine site and the contemporary metropolis. The design of these mines is linked to the gold price: when the resource price is high it becomes more cost effective to mine lower concentrations of ore. When the gold price is low, the mine is much smaller and located around the actual ore body and the higher concentrations of the ore body. So you have this condition where the real-time 3D models of each day's excavations are linked to the gold price. So one can see the new canyons that are carved out of this mythical landscape as actually being a real-time model or graph of the gold price.

The 'superpit' mine in Western Australia, 'a real-time model of the gold price'.

And the gold price itself is actually also a kind of fictional story. Despite the great lengths we go to to mine this stuff, for the most part what happens is we get the gold out of the ground just to quantify it; we section some of it off for industry and electronics, and the rest of it goes around to the other side of the world and gets buried in a bank vault. You have this situation where we go to huge expense, cutting up the Australian landscape, pulling out these resources only to smelter them down only to put them in another hole in the ground in a vault under HSBC in London. And then the gold is traded virtually. Gold itself is, besides its conductive value, a particularly useless material – it has only developed a value based on the evolution of its relationship with culture across

The Educator of Excess

time because it exists in a particular quantity, which shifts between rarity and abundance.

What you have is this contemporary economic fiction carved out of a landscape of mythical and traditional fictions about its creation, except it's no longer about rainbow serpents, it's about stock prices.

RH: It's both fascinating and depressing in equal terms.

LY: Exactly, but it's too easy to dismiss these situations as simple dystopian destruction because we do so from a heated room, from a building made of steel, while we chat on Skype and book our next low-cost holiday. We are all complicit and active agents in the anthropocenic, and it's not going to end suddenly. So what we have to do is find new ways we can start to culturally relate to this condition. And an aim of Unknown Fields is to prototype those sorts of things, and to acknowledge the complexity that exists there. It's easy to take a moral high ground by saying 'These things are wrong, we should stop mining', but that's not good enough. Being in this position where we can synthesise these complex factors, it's our role to acknowledge the complexity, and to explore new ways to start to navigate through it.

RH: It sounds like a very overwhelming but also productive terrain for thinking about architecture, and a strange and expansive experience for students preparing to enter the workforce. What kinds of places do they go on to work for? I can't imagine many of them end up in corporate firms designing office buildings.

LY: Well, some of them do actually. You have this amazing situation in London where at the end of your exhibition guys from Foster's office are walking around with their business cards poaching top students. And half of our studio got offers from them.

RH: In a way it makes sense. Foster, despite his reputation as the architect of choice for the corporate elite, has a slightly more radical heritage in British High-Tech, and having worked for Fuller for instance. He's even just rebuilt a Dymaxion car...

LY: I guess, but what I would like to think is that they are recognising students who are mature as designers with an independent voice, who are able to be clever and strategic about how they operate as designers. And at a place like Foster's, which is dealing with the complexities of building cities in China for instance, having someone who can think and operate at a strategic level is valuable to them. So we have people who go off to do stuff like that, but some students are also looking to develop new forms of practice themselves; some go on to become journalists; some have ended up doing concept design work for film and television; and we've had one who's gone off to set up and run the new research arm of Farshid Moussavi's new office for instance.

RH: What all these different destinations point to is a studio as a platform for exploring options beyond the largely unquestioned step from architecture school to working in an office. It acknowledges the precarity of employment today, where there is no longer the same job stability, where it seems everybody needs to develop their own brands and own websites to promote themselves straight from university.

LY: Our role as tutors is to equip the students with the skills to be able to do that. So often a school is caught up with ideas of what architects are supposed to be, without acknowledging how they actually have to operate in the world. We do classes on professional practice which are about contracts and liability, but we don't do classes on email writing, which is my dominant form of practice. We don't do classes on how to write a successful grant application. We don't do classes on defining a brand and creating a niche for yourself. So we try to use the studio as a place to develop strategies by which they can work independently as designers when they leave us.

And hopefully they can go out into the world without this reliance on making buildings. To talk about the different sorts of futures you can have now in architecture is just the responsible thing to do as an educator; that you can go off and design buildings with Foster's, but you can also go and curate exhibitions, write articles or be a research consultant. To just leave them to figure that out for themselves, and not allow them to test it within the freedom and experimental, supportive environment of an architectural school seems negligent. For architects to teach students that everything is going to be fine, and that they are going to go out to become a design intern in an architectural office, is just nuts.

RH: Do you have any desire to return to that territory, to buildings? You've been out there now, you've been on the experimental edge of the AA and Unknown Fields – what sort of project or brief would tempt you back to doing a building? If any?

LY: What I would argue for, is that our move away from building is not a diversion from architectural practice, it's not an excursion away from the core of what we do – it's just that we've defined the core of what we do in a particular way. I believe what we do is architecture, I believe what we do should be at the core of the profession. That is what the think-tank is about. It's not to say that these experimental forms of practice in some way down the line inform a more traditional form of practice; that would be privileging the physical building as the central point of what architects do, which I don't think is right anymore.

For us I don't see a move back into real building as it's been defined; that is a regression. We need to be much more vocal about staking a claim for these new positions, these new modes of operating as being part of the mainstream. It's fun to be a young designer talking about alternative forms of practice, but at some point I need to buy a house, I need to have kids, I need to put them through school. I don't want us to remain on the fringes.

THE
EDITOR
OF THE
BEYOND

Arjen
Oosterman
& Lilet
Breddels
Volume

'The typical architecture office generates a sad form of knowledge. The process of realizing a building produces idiosyncratic expertise, particularly in the uniqueness of local conditions – architecture, politics, contractors, history… But by the project's end, it is already clear that the architect's prodigious knowledge will never be reinvested in new, even more subtle projects in the same environment. We always have to move on, to the next frontier of unfamiliarity. We also become "experts" in typologies that we will never be asked to repeat'.[41]

It is with this statement of frustration that Rem Koolhaas introduces the first issue of *Volume* magazine in 2005. Despite the negativity of this passage, perhaps it also contains some implicit *hope*; hope that this nascent title could help redress

The triumvirate of *Volume* protagonists: Rem Koolhaas (AMO), Mark Wigley (C-Lab), Arjen Oosterman (Archis) and Jeffrey Inaba (C-Lab) in discussion at the launch of *Volume #24*: 'Counterculture'.

this issue of architectural knowledge and its inevitable evaporation.

Forged out of the ashes of *Archis*, a magazine with Dutch roots stretching back over 80 years,

Arjen Oosterman & Lilet Breddels

Volume was created as a new vehicle for the exploration of architectural ideas 'beyond' practice and its limitations.[42] The three founding protagonists – Archis Publishers, OMA's research think-tank AMO and Columbia University's C-Lab – each represent a unique aspect of architectural production to shape the magazine's agenda. Acting together as a network, these various partners are each plugged into different sources of knowledge and ideas.

Where most architectural magazines merely document the outcomes of architectural labour – buildings – *Volume* seeks to actively inform the issues architecture is concerned with through the creation and dissemination of knowledge. It promotes an architecture that is *informed*, that responds to *context*, and that produces the information necessary for architects to *act*. These conditions for action are geographically diverse, such as the Gulf region of the Middle East explored through two issues of *Al Manakh* (2007, 2010); promote different modes of operating, such as acting without a client ('Unsolicited Architecture', 2007); contribute to post-conflict scenarios ('Architecture of Peace', 2011); explore emergent territories for architectural speculation, such as new technologies ('Internet of Things', 2011) or a world after the challenge of sustainability has been 'solved' ('After Zero', 2008).

While *Volume* might *explore* all these various adjacent contexts for architecture, how can a magazine *be* a potential future for practice? As is discussed in the following interview, *Volume* is not the only product of Archis the publisher, which also includes Archis Interventions, a not-for-profit focused on events and exhibitions; Archis Tools, a consultancy arm advising on public engagement; and the SEE Network, which develops planning legislation in the post-conflict states of south-eastern Europe. In this sense, the contribution of the magazine doesn't end when it arrives on the newsstand. Unlike the 'sad form of knowledge' produced by the typical office, *Volume* presents ideas able to be deployed in new and unusual territories, expanding the possibilities for what architecture can offer.

Conducted 1st November 2011 at the offices of Archis in Amsterdam.

Rory Hyde: Let's start at the top: what led you to start *Volume*? What space did you identify within the landscape of magazines which you thought needed to be filled?

Arjen Oosterman: I think first of all, it was an awareness that architecture needed to be reconnected to the social domain. There's a sense of real irritation

Arjen Oosterman & Lilet Breddels

with the whole 'starchitecture' reality underpinning the start of *Volume*. And also a sense that the societal relation of the architect and of architecture seemed to be lost; there was no *deal* any more, no subject, no discussion.

RH: The other hint to the magazine's agenda is on the spine: 'to beyond or not to be'. It suggests that in order to get out of this internalised, anti-social, or starchitecture discussion, you need to get out of architecture itself. What do you mean by 'beyond'? Is it about looking beyond the usual urban, Western territories with which architecture generally concerns itself? Or is it about looking beyond in a more philosophical sense?

AO: I think there was a sense of the imminent death of architecture involved. The death of architecture has been proclaimed many times over the past century, and maybe even before that, but it was the loss of relevance and especially the loss of a political dimension that was dramatically apparent. So there was this sense – more than a hunch, an analysis – that architecture had to change. Then the first question becomes, 'What directions could and should be explored?' And that was the start of the 'beyond' adventure; it's about looking for territory and new domains for architecture. And then the other question is, 'What does society *ask* from architecture? What are the *needs* for architecture?' This dual process of exploration, research and reflection is what defines the project of going beyond.

RH: It's interesting, as in a way looking beyond became a kind of future prophesy. In the issue 'Crisis! What Crisis?'from 2006 you map out practically the *exact* trajectory the US housing collapse would follow, and the social and economic blowback that we're seeing now.[43] Back then, in the midst of the boom, it seemed like doomsaying, but now it seems remarkably prescient. Do you see a viable future for architecture outside of serving the top one percent? Outside of this very dependent discipline we've built around money? Are there alternatives, and is that the other agenda of the magazine perhaps?

Lilet Breddels: I think your question relates to whether architecture can play a role in changing a political or a societal system, or even in changing the world? And I do think it has a lot to do with

Volume #9 anticipated the US housing crisis in 2006, years before it would catastrophically collapse.

who you are catering to as an architect, who you are working for, and what your goal and target group are. For a long time of course that has been the commissioner. And at some point the commissioner turned out to be very big private corporations, which again led to starchitecture, and the rest was left to groups of building architects catering to the mass market who are not taken very seriously. So long before this crisis came along, we had another conception of what architecture is for, and to whom it is supposed to cater. And when you start to think like that, you immediately encounter other target groups, other non-Western countries, and other kinds of architecture.

My background is more in the art world, which in the 1990s started to look more to the outside world, instead of to their own internal realm; it started to open up to societal issues and to working in public space. But at the same time in the architecture world, it looked like the total opposite was happening, which for me was very strange because architecture has, in my view, always been more directly relatable to society, because you are working for people. Art can afford to be withdrawn internally into itself, but for architecture it is impossible, as it is still an applied art. You are doing it for people; they live in it, they work in it, and they move through it.

RH: The next question, then, is who is your target audience, and how do you use this platform to try and shift this conversation? Is it about reaching practising architects to try and encourage them to reconsider their terrains of operation? Or are you reaching out to an audience which is also beyond architecture? Is it more about a cultural shift in that sense, in terms of educating commissioners and the public about what architecture can be?

LB: That is certainly our hope, and our target group in that sense. I think if we really look at it, we have more influence still on architects and young professionals who are starting their careers and are looking for different ways of treating their profession, and for them we can be really inspirational. But I think that when you write you edit and create something, which you do when you make a magazine, you hope to reach a lot of people with your ideas. And we certainly do hope to reach people who have something to say, who have power, who are commissioners, who are potential clients, and who are policy makers. The political realm is very important for us, but maybe we don't reach them enough…

RH: It's probably worth noting at this point that you produce more than just a magazine as a platform for distributing ideas. Archis is a publisher, an organiser of exhibitions and events, and also a research lab. Is that the model, to use different platforms to reach different audiences?

> AO: The magazine is still a very useful and brilliant machine to not only bring together knowledge but also to produce knowledge; it actively produces ideas and new understanding for ourselves and for the people that are involved, and in the end for the reader we hope. And that's nice, but if we think we should stop collecting and start acting, then the other formats come into view, like events or exhibitions, or organising a conference. And ultimately collaboration is at the core of what we do. So, it's not just about advocating a message; it's very much about discovering what can be done and what should be done, and how it can be done by collaborating with different people and groups.

RH: The model of the organisation is also interesting from that perspective. I was personally surprised by the scale of the operation when compared to its cultural contribution; it's basically just four of you plus a few interns. That relates to this self-conception of Archis as a 'network', as a node within a larger set of people with different expertise and different backgrounds which you can tap into. How does that network structure enable different kinds of outcomes than if you were one big internalised institute for instance?

> AO: In a way it reflects the broader changes in modes of production currently underway. That is to say, the conception of the architect as 'master builder' or as 'grand master' in charge of the whole process is really an old-fashioned idea about how the built

Arjen Oosterman & Lilet Breddels

environment comes about. If we don't limit the definition of architecture to the built environment, but have a larger understanding of that notion, then it becomes even more interesting and even more important to change the way of working, and collaboration is essential to that. Situations are simply too complex nowadays to think that you can properly control the outcome and the solution on your own. Even the whole notion of a 'solution' is something to challenge.

So we find people who are knowledgeable in particular fields, and who bring their own expertise to collaboratively find out what can and should be done. It's similar to what you see with younger offices nowadays who don't profile themselves by saying 'We're school builders' or 'We're great with towers', but they instead promote a degree of intelligence they can bring to a situation or their ability to collaborate. In a way this is also how we work.

RH: The other key point of distinction is that each issue of *Volume* focuses on a particular theme. How do you choose the themes? Is it because they are relevant to architecture, or because they ought to be? Is it a reflection or a projection?

Volume #2 (2005) examined issues of agency and production. 'How do we define doing too much, too little? How to think through doing anyway?'

AO: Well, if you take architecture as a larger notion than building buildings seriously, then you have to clarify that, and then themes come to the fore. They might not yet be part of the architectural debate, but indeed should be. So in that sense we're putting them on the agenda, we hope.

RH: What's interesting is the kind of thinking that that lets you explore. The traditional trajectory of a magazine might be to document the *now*: the latest projects, the latest news, the latest ideas; and it's monthly to try to keep up with the pointy edge of time. But stepping out of that obligation to document the now, and focusing on issues, paradoxically allows you to look further forward and further afield.

AO: The disappointing thing about documenting the present – sure it's important to do and I don't want to challenge the relevance of any other magazines, I think they're very necessary as part of the profession – is that you discover that you're actually not documenting the present, you are documenting the past. Although the project might still be fresh, with the concrete still wet, the project was conceptualised five years ago. So you are discussing something that went on five years ago and then dealing with it as though it is the present day. Well it's not, and that kind of dragging behind reality was another reason why we thought we should step out of that kind of logic.

RH: Just to return to this idea of the role of the architect, the issue on 'Unsolicited Architecture' is perhaps the most explicit promotion of a new model for practice.[44] I'm interested in your thoughts in putting this together; did you see it as a provocation or as a viable alternative which would naturally be taken up?

LB: At the time it might have been provocative, as it sometimes still is, but it wasn't meant as a provocation. We explicitly intended to explore it as a viable option, and not just as a viable option for the *survival* of the profession – which was a large part of the discussion at that point – but as a means to return *responsibility* to the profession by setting an agenda and to really define the commission, the question, the need, and the ambition for society.

RH: I like this word 'responsibility', because as an architect you find this strange paradox in the shift from your training to your professional life.

As students we're presented with these grand social schemes by Le Corbusier or Hertzberger or Aldo van Eyck; of architecture that is inherently directed to achieving social aims, about improving something, or addressing a need. Then when you begin your internship or first job you inevitably

T-shirt issued by Archis. The dispiriting reality of starting a career in architecture.

work under very constrained briefs for very market-oriented proposals. It can be quite a shock. 'Unsolicited' seems to be a way to shortcut that moment of disillusionment that many young architects encounter, and which leads to many leaving the profession.

AO: I often think practice and education are completely unrelated. During education you are constantly asked to formulate your own project, and the moment you enter practice the clients are completely dictating *what* has to be done and even *how* it can be done. So this disconnect is also part of the inspiration to propose unsolicited-ness as an approach. And of course, it is also a rhetorical figure in a sense that by shifting back responsibility to the architect, even if it doesn't immediately produce a completely new practice, it will at least produce an awareness that the architect could perhaps meddle around with what the client asks, and could have an ambition of his or her own. That dimension was quite an important part of the professional logic of the 1950s and 1960s, where there was an internal debate going on – and the precursors to this magazine were instrumental in that – which was lost by and large through the 1970s and 1980s. By the early 2000s you are in this situation that this professional exchange on what architecture can bring to society is simply not happening at all. The model of the unsolicited architect was an attempt to maybe break that open.

LB: What we also encountered in making that issue is that if you go in and find your own urgencies or opportunities, then you also need to drastically rethink what kind of people you have in your office. You would need financial expertise, you would need a sociologist, a social geographer, all kinds of different people. So this idea of our own practice as a collaborative network which we talked about earlier also plays a very important role in the conception of the new architectural office. Collaboration is a huge issue: everyone talks about it, everyone wants it, and everyone says it needs to be done, but it's hugely difficult. Even after fifteen years of so-called multidisciplinary practice there are still today extremely separate worlds in which disciplines operate. And that also goes back to education, because the

departments are so separate. There is change,
of course, but it goes very slowly, and it's not easy.

RH: Hopefully that's the difference between how we
reclaim this social responsibility and ambition today,
compared to the 1950s and 1960s utopian project
which was delivered in a very top-down way; to shift
from the welfare-state model of social change to a
more networked and collaborative model, and yet still
retain this social ambition. That's hopefully the
moment we're in today.

> LB: I think if you dig into that further, this develop-
> ment of collaborative practice – of real collaboration,
> of real exchange – is definitely a future. It's also
> related to the digital age and the different views on
> authorship it brings – co-producing, pro-suming, that
> kind of thing – and it's big. I do agree with you that
> we are in a kind of pivotal moment.

RH: Which also leads to different expectations from
society and power.

> AO: And even to a shift in the self-image of archi-
> tects. What we discovered in the workshops with com-
> puter programmers and architects that we did for the
> 'Internet of Things' issue, is that programmers are a
> different species really; they don't feel the same
> authorship as architects do.[45] Architects completely
> identify with their product: 'Look at that building,
> I did that'. And that's the way they advertise their
> practice, it's a very logical model. In economic terms,
> architects deliver a service, but in societal terms they
> produce products. Whereas coders can't say 'I was
> responsible for this product'; that would be ridiculous,
> because much of what they do is collaborative. So
> their pride and satisfaction is different; it's about a

The Editor of the Beyond

communal effort, the joy of making something change or happen or start, and that requires a very different mentality or attitude towards your own practice or role within society, but also has consequences for the way you operate. Which immediately raises this counter-question: is there any satisfaction in working unsolicitedly, or working in these processes where you're not as visible as you are used to?

LB: In that sense, in the forthcoming issue on privatisation we are thinking a lot about sharing, and the notion of sharing becomes more and more important, from very down-to-earth, with car-sharing, sharing knowledge, sharing authorship, to sharing space in a mental way. The established hierarchies are dissolving.

THE ENVIRONM ENTAL MEDIC

Natalie Jeremijenko

xClinic

Environmental crisis is the greatest challenge facing our age, yet our response to it is far from clear. Pioneering environmentalists have urged us to think big and reshape our capacity for planetary-scale action by developing new disciplines, from Buckminster Fuller's re-conception of the planet as 'Spaceship Earth', all of us as astronauts, to Stewart Brand's 'Whole-Earth Discipline' of hybrid design-scientists. Although heroic, this line of thinking leaves us daunted and overwhelmed by the scale of the task, paralysed by inaction and tempted by apathy. How can we as individuals ever make a difference?

As Natalie Jeremijenko explains, 'the climate crisis has revealed to us a second and more pervasive crisis: the crisis of agency. Somehow, buying a local lettuce, changing a light bulb or driving at the speed limit doesn't seem sufficient to solve our climate crisis'.[46] Jeremijenko's response has been to establish the Environmental Health Clinic, a service offering individual 'prescriptions' for changes to personal environments, and the potential for widespread, aggregated change. Based at New York University (NYU), where Jeremijenko is Associate Professor of Art, the Environmental Health Clinic inverts the typical model of the health clinic by focusing

Natalie Jeremijenko

on the external conditions of the body, rather than our internal biology and genetic predispositions. Patients present their symptoms to the clinic, but instead of prescribing pharmaceuticals, Jeremijenko and her team prescribe actions aimed at improving environmental health.

The No Park returns greenery and permeability to a parking space reserved for access to a fire hydrant.

Actions have included the No Park, which returns a parking space reserved for access to a fire hydrant back to a more natural state by introducing plants and mosses, capturing polluted water before it reaches waterways and bringing greenery into urban streetscapes. The Farmacy Ag Bags are flexible green pockets for agricultural use, hung over railings or on windows to increase the city's productive capacity. More ambitious is the Urban Space Station, a symbiotic parasite placed on top of buildings in dense urban environments, which generates energy, contains a productive farm and treats the excess air and waste of its host. When I spoke with Jeremijenko, she was in Australia presenting her latest project, the Cross(×)Species

Adventure Club, a series of dinners exploring the 'gastronomical web' of human and non-human food ecosystems.

Each of these actions are based on the simple premise that if our environments are healthier then we will be too, leading directly to a focus on very urban-scaled issues of public space, urban ecosystems and the relationships between the people and animals within them. And although these actions are framed in a way that they are responses to an individual health symptom, their power is derived from the capacity to produce collective benefits. It is 'public health' in the most literal sense.

With a background in science, engineering and art, Jeremijenko's expertise goes far beyond the design disciplines as they are traditionally understood. Describing what she does as 'socio-ecological systems design', her practice offers a fascinating model for how to tackle the key challenges of the 21st century, without losing touch with the people who will change it.

Conducted 29th November 2011 over Skype between Amsterdam and Melbourne.

Rory Hyde: You seem to be in fairly ambiguous disciplinary territory – a kind of hybrid of artist, scientist, environmentalist and performer. What do you call yourself?

Natalie Jeremijenko

Natalie Jeremijenko: I call myself whatever it's strategic to call myself. It's often not useful to call yourself an artist, because as an artist you're just not credible in an environmental context. The phrase 'Artists say that global warming is...' is not credible. As a group, we can't even say we're professionals – there's no credentials or expertise – but I also think that's an advantage in many contexts. You're only as persuasive as your representations, and you get to stand in for the 'everyman' – if a 'dumb artist' can figure out these very complex socio-technical socio-ecological phenomena, then it must make sense. But I'm not interested in calling myself an architect – I don't think that's strategic.

RH: This is the trouble, actually. Calling yourself an architect is really a death sentence – it's like we're the guys who just make things look pretty because that's what we like, not because it's useful, and we make things really expensive. It's really the most useless claim to make.

NJ: It's certainly not useful for the sort of funding I get or projects I develop, although I really enjoy working with architects. For example, we installed a roof at the Postmasters Gallery in Chelsea about six years ago, which was infrastructure and facilities for high-density bird cohabitation, a model urban development with seven high-density housing complexes. This was architect-designed – we invited seven different firms to develop high-density housing for birds. The idea was to work at a 'real scale' for ecological and functional feedback, as opposed to the megalomaniac kind of architectural model that allows you to play God. I thought it was really funny. Anyway, I like working with architects, and I do build very close relationships

The Environmental Medic

with architectural co-conspirators, but I do understand the constraints of the profession somewhat.

RH: You do seem to be increasingly working on an urban and architectural scale, particularly with the UP_2_U project. Does it take a systems approach to the urban environment?

NJ: Yes. The project is for the Noguchi Museum, where four artists were invited to develop urban plans for Long Island City. It's a really interesting part of New York City because it's got the biggest housing projects in the area and the highest concentration of manufacturing left in the city. Working with landscape architect Peter Walker from JPW and architectural theorist Nina Rappaport, our approach is focused on creating 'vertical urban factories', where instead of expelling the manufacturing to the sprawling edges of cities, we facilitate it through industrial ecology. In a dense urban context, you can organise the inputs and outputs of energy and material flows much more effectively to create new opportunities and new incentive structures. I think it's fundamental.

For example, if you have a commercial bakery, you can use waste from the neighbourhood to heat the building – the incentives are aligned. I just don't want my kids exposed to emissions on their way to school. So, it actually structures the incentive in the correct ways. But a city is much more than an efficient machine to be tuned for minimising waste and maximising energy efficiency. We're also interested in the cultural opportunities, and how we can improve environmental health as a shared common good.

So one of the projects we're exploring is to retrofit the housing project blocks with room-less elevators.

You extend the elevator shaft thirty percent above the building in glass, so you can go up to see the incredibly charismatic New York skyline, and because it's glass, you also create natural ventilation, lessen the HVAC loads and improve the indoor air quality. In Manhattan, eighty percent of the carbon footprint is building related, and a lot of that is big HVAC systems that are flushing indoor air with outdoor air once every twenty minutes, on the ridiculous presumption that outdoor air quality is always better than indoor air quality. Indoor, you might have your formaldehyde and benzene and volatile organic compounds, but outdoors you've got particulates and mercury and carbon monoxide, and so you spend all this building energy mushing that all out.

RH: Air quality seems to be a critical aspect of your environmental health work. In your lectures you mention some incredible statistics – alarming rates of asthma, cancer, obesity – which all effectively relate to airborne pollutants. Are we just allergic to modern life? Is the solution to make our cities more like the nature we came from?

NJ: I don't think it's about any sentimental or nostalgic view of nature. There's a great quote from Einstein: 'Look deep into nature, and then you will understand everything better'. I think we have a lot to learn from natural systems, and I suppose my framework is to show how we can reframe environmental issues outside of the globalised discourse of global warming and global loss of biodiversity. In the last thirty years, the environmental movement has had to work really hard to make slow and imperceptible environmental changes newsworthy: 'Save the

The Environmental Medic

certainly not enough to support you, but it does give you the capacity to explore the wonder of flight.

So it's not about terror or speed or height or 'I'm going to die', but actually much more about the wonder of flight we all have, and to be able to explore and exploit that, to imagine ourselves in three-dimensional space instead of just shuffling about on the ground level. In Toronto, I would say this created a spectacle, a shared public memory for a possible future. And the kids were there to see it. They wouldn't let us fly the children, but they're the ones who started a petition that they wanted to fly to school – they would make arguments about how they're designing their own wings.

RH: How does flying on these zip lines fit into your agenda of environmental health?

NJ: Well, using a powered zip line with high RPM and regenerative braking, you can effectively be energy neutral. So in a building manufacturing context, in Long Island City, which is underserved by public transportation, what I'm planning to build – wish me luck on this! – is a zip line from Socrates Park to the nearest subway station a kilometre away, so people can fly with their wings to the train.

But what really holds the most potential is integrating this concept with the industrial urban ecosystem of Long Island City. Take just one commercial bakery in the area, say Tomcat Bakery, which does this delicious, airy artisanal bread delivered all around New York City. Every morning, seventy-six trucks roll up and idle around for hours, releasing huge amounts of diesel fumes, which we know causes asthma and compromised cardiovascular health in all of us. That burden is unfairly borne by the local

residents. Now, with a micro power plant connected to the new extended elevators I discussed before, we could run zip lines down to the waterfront to zip the goods about, obviating the needs for these idling trucks. It's quiet, fast, emission free, inexpensive and would form a palpable spectacle of urban life and activity.

RH: To return to the question of your role, you seem to have invented this new discipline of 'environmental medic' – a kind of hybrid artist/architect/scientist/engineer – largely abandoning the art and design disciplines as they currently exist. Are the traditional disciplines ineffective for what we need to achieve?

NJ: I actually think my work is quite specific, although it does look like it comes from all over the place. It's really *socio-ecological systems design*. I don't know if this is a prescription for all designers, but I certainly think that part of the work of problem-forming – as opposed to problem-solving, which designers pride themselves on – is really about thinking through the challenges that we face in the 21st century: re-imagining our urban infrastructures, promoting biodiversity, getting beyond 19th-century hygiene myths. We need to further apply ideas of biodiversity and complexity – not towards LEED points or awards, but towards possibilities that are very specific, particular and local, and that can aggregate for significant effect.

I do think that the service structure of the design professions is very limiting, that figuring out what the problems are outside of commissions is a big challenge. If someone isn't telling you what to do or what needs building, then you have to develop your own problems to solve, and I think the opportunity to do

that is something that designers could do and are seizing much more. I call what I do 'x-design' – experimental design – but maybe it should be called 'o-design', because it's very opportunistic in the sense that it's about framing the problem.

RH: Do we need to be more opportunistic or transgressive?

NJ: Well, the other really important aspect is technology: every new technology is an opportunity for social and environmental change. Of course, it's usually a profoundly conservative force because technology is by definition resource intensive – large companies, governments and the military have the resources to develop and deploy technologies in their own interests. But the other good thing about using technology as a medium is that it's too complex, it has all these unintended consequences that I think can be seized as opportunities. So fundamentally, if there was a design methodology that I use, it's to examine new technologies for their capacity for social and environmental change.

Urban Space Station, a symbiotic parasite providing food and clean air to high-rise buildings.

Interior of scale model of Urban Space Station, Reina Sofia Museum Madrid.

The other thing is, when you're not working for some big engineering firm getting charged out at five hundred dollars an hour, you're actually able to formulate other strategies which might be more

Natalie Jeremijenko

participatory or more open. The Urban Space Station is designed to be assembled as a barn-raising, precisely because it's designed for the common good; intensified food production in an urban context has a benefit for shared air quality, water quality and environmental health. It's in everyone's interest. To build it as a barn-raising is obviously much less expensive, but it's also so that the motley crew of students who build it can understand it, and know how to maintain it, and also know how to make it better next time. It's a collective response to the collective problem of food production in an urban context.

Participatory research, participatory construction and open source: these are all strategies under my belt that I think are critically important for contemporary design, and they aren't the ones necessarily taught in architecture schools.

ENDNOTES

Foreword

1   Kevin Lynch, *The Image of the City*, MIT Press, 1960.
2   Malcolm MacEwan, *Crisis in Architecture*, RIBA Publications, 1974.
3   Anthony Carnevale, Ban Cheah *et al.*, *Hard Times: College Majors, Unemployment and Earnings*, Georgetown University Centre for Education and the Workforce, 2011. http://www9.georgetown.edu/grad/gppi/hpi/cew/pdfs/Unemployment.Final.pdf.
4   Rem Koolhaas, 'Beyond the Office', *Volume #1*, 2005.
5   Norman Potter, *What is a Designer*, Studio Vista, 1969.

Introduction

6   Thomas Zung (ed.), *Buckminster Fuller: Anthology for a New Millennium*, St Martin's Press, 2002.
7   Bruce Mau, 'Design and the Welfare of All Life' in Tilder, L. and Blostein, B. (eds.), *Design Ecologies: Essays on the Nature of Design*, Princeton Architectural Press, 2010, p. 12.
8   Paola Antonelli, *Design and the Elastic Mind*, New York, Museum of Modern Art, 2008, p. 17.
9   John Thackara, *In the Bubble: Designing in a Complex World*, MIT Press, 2005, p. 7.

Bruce Mau

10   Bruce Mau, 'You Can Do Better', *Architect*, 2011.
11   Bruce Mau, *Massive Change,* Phaidon, 2004.
12   Bruce Mau, 'Nielson Design Lecture', State Library of Queensland, 2011. http://www.slq.qld.gov.au/find/webcasts/nielson.

Indy Johar

13   00:/, 'Compendium for the Civic Economy', Nesta and Design Council CABE, 2011.
14   Indy Johar, presentation as part of 'And Now What:

Rethinking Spatial Practice During Crisis', Architecture Foundation, London, 2009. http://vimeo.com/5987779.
15   Indy Johar, 'Time to Start Reading the Financial Papers', 2009. http://www.world architecturefestival.com/news-detail. cfm?newsId=92.
16   http://www.fintrydt.org.uk.

Reinier de Graaf & Laura Baird

17   Rem Koolhaas, 'Contents', in Rem Koolhaas and Brendan McGetrick (eds.), *Content*, Taschen, 2004, p. 20.

Mel Dodd

18   Timothy Moore and Rory Hyde, 'Keeping the Pace: Interview with Esther Charlesworth', *Volume #26:* Architecture of Peace, Archis, 2010.

Wouter Vanstiphout

19   Wouter Vanstiphout, 'Blame the Architect: On the Relationship between Urban Planning, Architecture, Culture and Urban Violence', Lecture at the Architecture Association, London, 3rd February 2010.
20   Crimson Architectural Historians, 'Maakbaarheid: Reinventing the Urban Project in Rotterdam' in Reiniets, T., Sigler, J. & Christiaanse, K. (eds.), *Open City: Designing Coexistence*, SUN, 2009.
21   Chad Friedrichs (dir.), *The Pruitt-Igoe Myth: An Urban History*, documentary film, 2011. www.pruitt-igoe.com.

Camila Bustamante

22   David Harvey, 'The Right to the City', *New Left Review*, no 53, 2008.
23   'Actions: What You Can Do With the City', Canadian Centre for Architecture, Montréal, 26th November 2008 – 19th April 2009.

Steve Ashton

24   John Macarthur, 'Australian Baroque: Geometry and Meaning at the National Museum of Australia', *Architecture Australia*, March/April, 2001.

Bryan Boyer

25   Bryan Boyer and Justin Cook, 'Clearing the Cowshed', *Perspecta: Failure,* 2012 (forthcoming).

Todd Reisz

26   www.pwc.com/en_M1/m1/industries/healthcare/healthcarebrochure.pdf.
27   Todd Reisz, 'Cities Solve Problems', in Rem Koolhaas, Todd Reisz, *et al.* (eds.), *Al Manakh 2: Gulf Continued,* Archis, 2010, p. 265.
28   Todd Reisz, 'As a Matter of Fact, The Legend of Dubai', *Log,* 13/14, 2008.
29   Redwan Zaouk interviewed by Joumana al Jabri, Todd Reisz and Reda Sijiny, 'City of Knowledge', in Rem Koolhaas, Todd Reisz, *et al* (eds.), *Al Manakh 2: Gulf Continued,* Archis, 2010, p. 266.
30   CBS News, 'A Visit to Dubai Inc.', *60 Minutes,* broadcast 14th October, 2007. http://www.cbsnews.com/2100-18560_162-3361753.html
31   Rory Hyde, 'Dubai Bashing', *op. cit.* *Al Manakh 2,* p. 68.

Marcus Westbury

32   Marcus Westbury, 'Fluid Cities Create', *Griffith Review,* 2008.
33   Marcus Westbury, 'Cities as Software', *Volume #27*: Ageing, Archis Publishers, 2011.

DUS Architects

34   Timothy Moore, 'Risky Living: Interview with Bart Lootsma', *Architecture Australia,* Nov/Dec, 2011.
35   Bart Lootsma, *SuperDutch: New Architecture in the Netherlands,* Princeton Architectural Press, 2000.

Jeanne Gang

36   Jeanne Gang, *Reverse Effect: Renewing Chicago's Waterways,* Studio Gang Architects, 2011.

Conrad Hamann

37   Statement by Robin Boyd in 1949, quoted in Geoffrey Serle, *Robin Boyd:* *A Life,* Melbourne University Press, 1996, p. 92.
38   Robin Boyd, *The Australian Ugliness,* Text Publishing, Melbourne, 2010 (1960), p. 74.
39   Robin Boyd, *Kenzo Tange,* G. Braziller, New York, 1962.
40   Gideon Haigh, interviewed on *The Architects,* Triple R, Melbourne, 2010.

Arjen Oosterman & Lilet Breddels

41   Rem Koolhaas, 'Beyond the Office', *Volume #1,* 2005.
42   History of Archis, accessed November 2011. http://www.archis.org/archis/archis-history.
43   *Volume #10*: Crisis! What Crisis? Suburbia after the Crash, Archis Publishers, 2006. Based on Alexander d'Hooghe's research and studio at MIT.
44   *Volume #14*: Unsolicited Architecture, Archis Publishers, 2007. Based on the work of a studio run by Ole Bouman at MIT.
45   *Volume #28*: Internet of Things, Archis Publishers, 2011.

Natalie Jeremijenko

46   Natalie Jeremijenko, 'The Art of the Eco-Mindshift', *TED Global,* lecture, 2009. http://www.ted.com/talks/natalie_jeremijenko_the_art_of_the_eco_mindshift.html.

IMAGE CREDITS

CONTRIBUTOR BIOGRAPHIES

Rory Hyde is a practising architect working across research, publishing, broadcasting, curation and building. He studied architecture at RMIT University in Melbourne, where he also completed a PhD on emerging models of practice enabled by new technologies. He is a contributing editor of *Architecture Australia*, and co-host of *The Architects*, a weekly radio show on architecture, which will be presented in the Australian pavilion in the 2012 Venice Architecture Biennale. Based in Amsterdam since 2009, Rory has worked with *Volume* magazine, MVRDV, the NAi, Viktor & Rolf and Mediamatic. roryhyde.com

Dan Hill is a strategic design lead at Sitra, the Finnish Innovation Fund, in Helsinki. An interaction designer by trade, he has previously been a design leader at Arup, Monocle, BBC, *Domus* and others. He is an Adjunct Professor in the Department of Architecture at University of Technology Sydney and a member of the advisory board of the Integrated Design Commission in South Australia. He has worked on major urban projects worldwide, and with Rogers Stirk Harbour + Partners, Shigeru Ban Architects, Carlo Ratti, Philippe Rahm, HASSELL and Donovan Hill, among others. cityofsound.com

Steve Ashton is a founding director of the Melbourne-based architecture and urban design practice Ashton Raggatt McDougall. He has extensive experience in high-level project management and business administration, including non-traditional techniques such as project alliancing. a-r-m.com.au

Laura Baird is an Associate of the international architecture and urbanism practice OMA, where she is a designer and researcher with AMO, the practice's Rotterdam-based research studio which operates beyond the traditional boundaries of architecture. oma.nl

Bryan Boyer is a strategic design lead at Sitra, the Finnish Innovation Fund, and project manager of the Helsinki Design Lab. helsinkidesignlab.org

Lilet Breddels is an art historian and the director of the Archis Foundation, a cultural think-tank dealing with spatial reflexivity and urban urgencies. Archis initiates projects and debates all over the world, and is the publisher of *Volume* magazine. archis.org

Camila Bustamante is a co-founder of La Factura, a Lima-based social enterprise operating across design, communication, strategy and transport. lafactura.com

Mel Dodd is a member of the socially-engaged art and architecture collaborative muf, and the founder of muf_aus, operating across socially engaged art practice, urban design, research, education and the public realm. She holds a PhD from RMIT University, where she is Associate Professor. muf.co.uk

DUS Architects was founded in 2004 by Hedwig Heinsman, Martine de Wit and Hans Vermeulen. DUS builds 'public architecture': architecture that influences the public domain using 1:1 scale models, urban processes and strategy design. dusarchitects.com

Jeanne Gang is founder and principal of Studio Gang Architects, a Chicago-based collective of architects, designers and thinkers whose projects confront pressing contemporary issues. She was awarded a MacArthur Fellowship in 2011. studiogang.net

Reinier de Graaf is a Partner of the international architecture and urbanism practice OMA, and director of AMO, the practice's Rotterdam-based research studio which operates beyond the traditional boundaries of architecture. oma.nl

Conrad Hamann is a widely-published architectural historian and lecturer and foremost expert on the work of Australian Modernist architects Robin Boyd, Roy Grounds and Frederick Romberg, the subjects of his doctorate.

Natalie Jeremijenko is Associate Professor of Visual Art at New York University, where she directs the Environmental Health Clinic, a clinic and lab which approaches health from an understanding of its dependence on external environments, rather than on the internal biology of an individual. environmentalhealthclinic.net

Indy Johar is co-founder of 00:/, a London-based strategy and design practice with a focus on architecture, economy, sustainability and society. architecture00.net

Bruce Mau is a world-leading visionary, innovator, designer and author. He is co-founder of the Massive Change Network and chairman emeritus and founder of Bruce Mau Design, with studios in Toronto and New York. massivechangenetwork.com

Arjen Oosterman is a writer, educator and the editor-in-chief of *Volume* magazine, an independent quarterly that goes beyond architecture's definition of 'making buildings' to reclaim the cultural and political significance of architecture. volumeproject.org

Todd Reisz is an architect and writer with a focus on the Gulf region. He is editor of *Al Manakh 2: Gulf Continued* which analyses the recent development of cities in Saudi Arabia, Kuwait, Qatar, Bahrain and the UAE. toddreisz.com

Wouter Vanstiphout is a founding partner of the Rotterdam-based research and planning studio Crimson Architectural Historians, and Professor of Design and Politics at the Delft University of Technology. crimsonweb.org

Matt Webb is CEO and Principal at BERG, a London-based strategy and product development studio which he co-founded in 2005. He is a regular speaker on the inspirational role of design and technology in culture. berglondon.com

Marcus Westbury is a writer, broadcaster, television presenter, festival director and founder of Renew Newcastle, a not-for-profit urban renewal scheme that brokers access to empty buildings for creative enterprises, artists and cultural projects in his hometown of Newcastle, Australia. renewnewcastle.org

Liam Young is a London-based architect and educator. He directs the Architecture Association's Unknown Fields Division, and is founder of Tomorrow's Thoughts Today, a think-tank exploring the consequences of fantastic, perverse and underrated urbanisms. tomorrowsthoughtstoday.com

INDEX

First published 2013 by Routledge,
711 Third Avenue, New York, NY 10017

Simultaneously published in the UK
by Routledge, 2 Park Square, Milton Park,
Abingdon, Oxon OX14 4RN

*Routledge is an imprint of the Taylor &
Francis Group, an informa business*

© 2013 Taylor & Francis

*Library of Congress Cataloging in
Publication Data*: A catalog record for this
book has been requested

ISBN: 978-0-415-53353-9 (hbk)
ISBN: 978-0-415-53354-6 (pbk)
ISBN: 978-0-203-10022-6 (ebk)

Printed in Spain by GraphyCems.

Transcription   Jude Crilly
Acquisition editor   Wendy Fuller
Editorial assistant   Laura Williamson
Production editor   Ben Woolhead
Design   Sam de Groot
Cover photography   Liam Tickner

Typeset in Digi Antiqua Light Condensed.
Publisher's note: This book has been
prepared from camera-ready copy by the
author.

Interview with Wouter Vanstiphout first
published in *Architecture Review Australia*.
Interview with Mel Dodd first published in
Architecture Australia.

ACKNOWLEDGEMENTS
The author would like to thank all those
who generously gave their time to be inter-
viewed, and to all those who gave their
ideas and feedback on the development of
this book: Sam de Groot, Jude Crilly,
Dan Hill, Bryan Boyer, Tobias Natrass
Pond, Mark Burry, Mat Ward, Simon
Sellars, Justine Clark, Timothy Moore,
Amelia Borg, Camilla Hornby, Stuart
Harrison, Simon Knott, Katja Novitskova,
Anthony and Chloe Hyde, Amy Silver.